Table of Contents

MW00570049

Acknowledgements

I would personally like to thank a few people who played a part in the success and actualization of this book. The key players who joined with me in the development of Austin's Best through High Mountain Publishing are Natalie Rupert and Bonnie Wilson. What a team they are! Without their dedication to the purpose and cause of Austin's Best, I would still be climbing up a very icy mountain. There is actually no way to say "thank you" enough to these two wonderful, extremely talented ladies.

In the beginning when this book was only a concept of what could be, my parents, Dr. William G. and Kerry Ellis, were there as usual to remind me that I could do whatever I dream of doing. They listened untiringly to me, and as usual were my sounding board. With their final "you can do it" words and a smile, I am now writing this page to say "thank you Mom and Dad." I am who I am because of you!

As for the beautiful artwork flowing from cover to cover, I would like to personally recognize Linda Dumont. What a treat to have met you and to uncover your unique and wholesome personality. Anyone who is able to enjoy your paintings is able to dance with the best.

As for an Austin treat, Jim Innes, you take the cake! From shooting the commercial to working on the photography in the book you have been quite fun. The future holds so much.

Jim Roberson...not just my CPA, not just my financial advisor, but my great supportive friend. You are so cool! It is so nice to have such support from a "bottom line" kind of guy.

Rosalinda Babin, Jeannie and Charlie Tuttle, Bill and Debbie Lee and David Buttross are my great friends who are there for me day or night to listen to my concerns, my excitement, as well as my day to day adventures. Thank you for being my friend who I can truly count on!

Tracy Wesch of Dog Trick Design and Kelly McDermott of Graphic Designs, both of whom are exceptional in their creative design work not to mention their ability to meet our deadlines, thank you.

Pam Postel and Melissa Kruckenberg both really knew how to keep us focused and on track without losing their cool. You have listened and worked so diligently without complaining. Your work ethic is greatly admired.

AUSTIN'S
BEST

An informative guide to the Austin area's most distinctive businesses, for newcomers, residents, and tourists.

Tama Ellis Adair

High Mountain
Publishing

Austin, Texas

Austin's Best

Copyright © 2000 by Tama Ellis Adair

First Edition
Published by:
High Mountain Publishing
4412 Spicewood Springs Rd
Austin, Texas 78759
(512) 345-9804   (877) 466-0415
Fax: (512) 338-0655

Contributing Editor, Tracy Staton
Vice President of Marketing, Bonnie Wilson
Director of Distribution, Natalie Rupert
Artwork by Linda Dumont, Copyright © 1999 Linda Dumont Studios
Photography by Jim Innes, Copyright © 1999 Jim Innes
Art Direction by Tracy Wesch, Copyright © Dog Trick Design
Map Design, Kelly McDermott ©
Printing by Press Corps, Inc.

Library of Congress Catalog Card Number
LCC 99-97123
Tama Ellis Adair
Tracy Staton
Austin's Best · First Edition · Austin, Texas

ISBN 0-9675270-0-7
Visit us online at:
http://www.austintravelguide.com
http://www.austinsbestguide.com

High Mountain Publishing
A Lady's Day Out In Austin and Surrounding Areas

Thank you Kelly White and Beth Atherton of Safe Place as well as Sandra Martin of Travis County Children's Advocacy Center Austin for allowing us to help in some way with your cause. You all work very hard in your endeavors to help single parents and children. My hat goes off to you and your staff as you daily walk through others trials and tribulations.

Collin Barnes, editor of Austin Monthly, thanks you for your support.

Mayor Kirk Watson, for the insight to the book and your continuous way of supporting Austin, the people of Austin, and the growth that brings us all new paths to walk in this capital city. I hope you enjoy the recognition that this book can and will bring to Austin.

The strongest link to a beautiful book, and one of my dearest long time friends, Tracy Staton, contributing editor. Your communication style is unsurpassed in the writing world. Your friendship alone has been such a special blessing because of the paths that we have walked together and then to think that one of our dreams has finally come true. We are now working partners in this endeavor of which I am very thankful! You told me years ago, we could and would write some-day, and here we are.

And finally, my most precious supporter in the world, my daughter Brooke. You are beautiful and full of energy at such a young age. You make me excited to do what I do everyday of my life. Thank you for supporting me. I love you, Sweetie.

From the Author:

Over the years, I have walked a great number of different paths and had the chance to see at least part of this big world. But the biggest blessing in my life was following the path that led me to Austin, Texas, two years ago. What a treat! I can honestly say that I have never experienced a city with as much excitement, as much culture, and as many warm and friendly people as I have discovered in this capital city.

I've started two companies in Austin, and I'm sure you'll agree that this city has a great entrepreneurial spirit. This town has been built through hard work and great creativity, and I'm glad to be a part of it. When I first arrived, my greatest desire when the demands of single motherhood and running a company permitted was to learn as much as I could about this wonderful city and experience it for myself.

So, what did I do first? I went to bookstores and scanned the shelves for anything I could find that would give me a look at Austin's history. Not just plain old history, but history that made me excited to go see and do; history that made me excited to tell my friends and family about our new home. It came to me that no one was really telling the stories of the true Austin. Austin is a beautiful city, but Austin is Austin because of the people.

This book is intended to help fill the gap on Austin. Here you'll find many of the people that are making a difference in Austin. People who are running vibrant, growing businesses. People who are creating art, directing movies, and writing new music. I hope that this book will inspire you to go and do and see, the way I have as my associates and I have put together this marvelous book on my favorite city.

Austin is unique, and deserves a unique look at what makes it so special.

Early Austin

In April 1839, the Third Congress of the Republic of Texas, headed by President Mirabeau B. Lamar, appointed Judge Edwin Waller to supervise the layout of a new capital city. Just seven months later, the 640-acre tract hosted the first session of the Fourth Congress of the Republic of Texas. From its earliest days in the Republic, through statehood, the Civil War and Reconstruction, in periods of growth as well as times of depression, this great city has always maintained its unique quality. As author John Henry Faulk once wrote, "Most people who have lived in Austin for any length of time tend to agree that it is about the primest town in Texas."

Since 1492, six flags have flown over Texas: France, Spain, Mexico, the Republic of Texas, the Confederate States of America, and the United States of America. The French and Spanish sparred back and forth for generations, both claiming ownership until 1721, when the Spanish established the province of Texas near the present day Robeline, Louisiana.

By 1821, Texas natives assisted the colony of Mexico in gaining independence from Spain. In return, the Mexican government granted the Texas natives large tracts of land with the provision that they would develop and populate their newly acquired land. It was during this same time that Stephen F. Austin established the headquarters of the first colony of Americans in Texas. For years, Stephen Austin was committed to keeping his American colonists citizens of Mexico. But as new pioneers spilled into Texas from Tennessee, Kentucky, Missouri, and other points in the young United States, the cry for Independence reached a crescendo in 1836, and Texans went to war for their freedom. After several battles culminated in the victory of San Jacinto, the Republic of Texas was established with Sam Houston serving as first president.

In 1839 Austin was designated as the new Republic's capital. It was during this time Mirabeau B. Lamar and a group of friends were camping near the Colorado River near a small community called Waterloo.

Lamar was so impressed by the beauty of the area that he recommended it as the perfect place for the nation's capital. Edwin Waller, one of the signers of the Texas Declaration of Independence, designed the new capital city. Some of the streets were named for native trees; some were named for Texas rivers.

The first capital building was located at the corner of Colorado and Hickory street. In October, Lamar, along with other officials and archives in a caravan of 50 wagons, arrived to conduct government business at this new site. In 1853 this capital building burned and a temporary structure was built until the legislature could come up with a plan to finance a building more fitting for Austin. A land-swapping plan was implemented which raised the needed funds. Today, residents as well as tourists still marvel at the beautiful pink granite building overlooking Congress Avenue.

Texas officially became the 28th state of the United States on February 19, 1846, with Austin at the helm as the capital. By 1840, Congress Avenue was lined with one-and two-story buildings. This started the first Austin boom which continues to exist on an even larger and more grandiose scale today.

During the past 160 years, Austin residents have built magnificient buildings such as St. David's Episcopal Church at the corner of 7th and San Jacinto. In 1854, a Greek revival mansion was authorized as the home for the governor.

It is hard to capture in print the vast beauty of the Austin area. The former first lady of Texas, Lucadia Niles Pease, declared, "I often ride in the carriage around the town, and there are beautiful drives in every direction."

Austin was not spared the violent effects of the Civil War. It, as well as other Texas towns, contributed their share of gray-uniformed men to fight for the Confederate cause. As in other parts of the country, the local economy was devastated by the war. It was not until the end of the 1860s that signs of recovery and prosperity started to crop up throughout the state.

From time to time, the Colorado River would flood the surrounding area. Finally, a stone bridge constructed in 1884 allowed development to take place along the south side of the river. Another important contributor to the growth and prosperity of Austin was the arrival of the Houston and Texas Central Railroad.

By 1875, Austin was home to the new Travis County limestone courthouse, a flourishing business district on Congress Avenue, and Barton Springs was becoming a favorite spot for family outings.

In 1881 Austin became the proud residence of the University of Texas. 40 acres of land located north of Capitol Square were allocated for the university. Today, the university is ranked among the top 25 universities in the country with many of their colleges ranking among the top 10. "Hook em Horns" can be heard throughout Austin on game day when the Longhorns play their home football games. The recently renovated Darrell K. Royal Texas Memorial Stadium is surrounded by beautiful sky boxes where alumni, corporate executives, and many other Texas fans enjoy the game in grand style.

Present Day Austin

Austin always manages to stay in the spotlight of the national press. Fortune magazine ranked Austin "The Best City for Business in North America" in its 10th annual ranking of America's preeminent business centers. Many factors contributed to Austin,s number one ranking, including the soaring number of high-tech start-up firms that call Austin home. Closer to home, Austin has a vibrant media sector. Austin Monthly, Texas Monthly, The Austin American-Statesman, and The Austin Business Journal are just a few of the publications available here.

Austin has also been named "Literacy City" for the most books sold on a per capita basis in the United States. This is not surprising, because every November The First Lady of Texas, Laura Bush, dons her hat as Honorary Chairperson, and Austinites gear up for The Texas Book Festival, the largest literary event in the state. The event sponsors Texas Public Libraries. Booksellers, publishers, and concession vendors donate a portion of their profits to the festival.

If you are a budding writer-and there are a lot of writers in Austin the Austin Writers League hosts monthly meetings featuring successful editors and writers as speakers. The League also sponsors workshops throughout the year, with subject matters ranging from poetry to technical writing.

Austin Arts

Austin has a world-class arts scene, featuring museums, galleries, and a year-round performing arts calendar. In the historic Hyde Park neighborhood you'll find the Elisabet Ney Museum, the former home of famous sculptress Elisabet Ney. The Museum features famous Texans such as Gen. Sam Houston and Stephen F. Austin. The University of Texas campus contains dozens of Texas-themed works as well. Works from the late sculptor, Charles Umlaf, whose pieces can be found in the Smithsonian and NewYork's Metropolitan Museum, can be found at the Umlaf Sculpture Garden & Museum. Located at the University of Texas is the Archer M. Huntington Gallery, which has a comprehensive selection of Latin American art and boasts the works of such names as Botero, Rembrandt, and Degas.

Entertainment

Austin Recreation Water and outdoor activities are abundant in Austin. You will find many Austinites enjoying the hike and bike trails that extend around Zilker Park, and when you visit the area lakes, you'll find water skiing, sailing, fishing, and even dinner cruises on an intimate riverboat. Of course, one of the most popular spots for sunbathers and swimmers in the summer is a 1,000 foot long natural pool known as Barton Springs. Swimmers flock here to enjoy its 68-degree water, a big plus considering that Austin can reach over 100 degrees in the heart of summer!

Austin Music

Austin is home to many music genres, and is internationally recognized as "The Live Music Capital of the World." Many well-known artists have called Austin their home, including Stevie Ray Vaughan, Janis Joplin, and Willie Nelson. With more than 100 clubs and other venues, Austin provides many styles of music, including blues, folk, rock, alternative, country, jazz, and Latino. One of the many ways to see live music in Austin is to cruise the clubs up and down Sixth Street, but you can also find many concert halls and outdoor stages in other locations.

Some places to check out: The Austin Music Hall, The Backyard, Frank Erwin Center/Bass Concert Hall, and the Paramount Theatre. Every March Austin hosts The South by Southwest Music and Media Conference and Festival, where thousands of aspiring musicians flood into Austin for a chance to be discovered.

Tour Information

Austin Convention And Visitors Bureau 201 E. 2nd St. 512/478-0098 or 800/926-2282
Planning a trip to Austin? The Convention and Visitors Bureau can help. When visiting the Bureau, you'll find a rich source of brochures on what to see and where to stay. Guided tours are one of their specialties. They are offered on weekdays and weekends from March through November.

Greater Austin Chamber of Commerce
111 Congress Avenue. 512/478-9383
When moving to Austin, call The Greater Austin Chamber of Commerce to receive a relocation packet. For business owners relocating, The Chamber offers extensive programs, initiatives, and volunteer committees.

Hispanic Chamber of Commerce of Travis County
823 Congress Ave 512/476-7502
The Hispanic Chamber of Commerce is a hub of information, offering Hispanic and Latin American conventions and visitor activities. Call them if you are a travel agency or tour operator, and they will provide you with plenty of tourist information.

Capitol Complex Visitors Center
112 E. 11th 512/305-8400
When visiting this fabulous 1888 historic site, self-guided and scheduled guided tours are available. For avid shoppers, The Capitol Gift Shop provides Texas memorabilia.

Central Austin

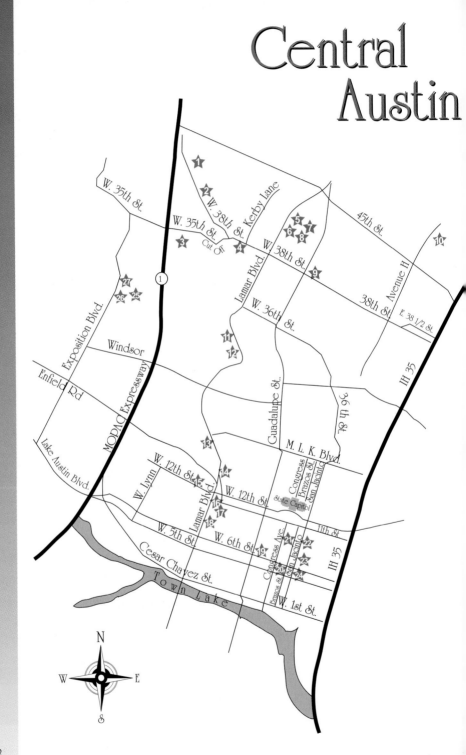

Sooner or later, everyone who wants to visit the "real" Austin has to come here. After all, you can't visit the Texas Capitol anywhere else, and shopping historic Sixth Street and its environs is a must. And if you want to sample Austin's legendary music scene, the bars and clubs in Central Austin are where it resides. Not to mention the dining. Central Austin houses a handful of truly upscale restaurants—some of the best in the city—and a host of great joints, from Tex-Mex to authentic deli.

1 The Menagerie.

This gallery of fine jewelry, sparkling crystal, gleaming silver and fine china had its beginnings in "twistie beads". Remember? They were all the rage in the late 1970s, and Vickie Roan started her business selling them from home. But at the prodding of friends, she branched out into diamonds, pearls and gemstones. And her business blossomed.

In 1994, she expanded into china, crystal and silver to become Austin's premier bridal registry shop. Now The Menagerie carries more than 200 different patterns of the world's finest tableware and barware, and boasts an exclusive-to-Austin arrangement with William Yeoward English crystal, Odiot sterling flatware from France, and Christofle china, crystal and silver.

It's not just the fabulous selection that makes The Menagerie a wonderful place to shop. It's also the attention to beauty here. Fresh flowers bloom all over the store. An array of sterling picture frames marches across the baby grand piano. A pianist coaxes music from the instrument on Saturday afternoons and holidays, a fitting accompaniment to shopping among the classically elegant merchandise.

To aid those shopping for wedding gifts, each bride's table settings are displayed next to a sterling frame containing their printed registry. Seekers of baby gifts will find them arranged within an antique secretary. And those browsing for jewelry can pull antique chairs up to the Louis XV jewelry cases.

Such devotion to detail extends to the meticulous service. The knowledgeable staff of nine delights in helping customers with their gift needs, whether a corporate order for 500 or a single christening keepsake. You'll quickly understand why "We are here to serve you" is the store motto. Once your selection is made, you'll be delighted to discover that gift wrap and Austin-area delivery are complimentary. And the service doesn't stop with one sale. Your personal gift enclosure cards may be kept on file, so The Menagerie will always be ready to send a gift on your behalf.

Roan says it best when she calls her store "a shop of happiness." Let The Menagerie spread some cheer your way today.

To find it: 1601 W. 38th Street, No. 7 Jefferson Square.
Phone: 512/453-4644, 800/778-4644.
Accepts: MC, Visa, Discove, AMEX. Personal checks.
Hours: 10 a.m. to 5:30 p.m. Monday to Saturday.
Notable: After-hours appointments available. Complimentary delivery. Bridal registry. Exclusives on William Yeoward crystal; Odiot sterling flatware; and Christofle flatware, china, crystal and giftware.

4 The Garden Room.

Every detail in this Jefferson Square shop—from the creative decor to the appealing mix of clothing, gifts and home decor—delights the senses. Unique clothing and gifts range from the classical to the whimsical, with such decorative lines as Mackenzie-Childs and the exclusive LTD home collection. Clothing from Votre Nom..., Bonnie Strauss, Rex Ghost, Eileen Fisher, and Whistles from London completes the mix of attitudes and styles.

To find it: No. 5 Jefferson Square, Kerbey Lane at 35th Street.
Phone: 512/458-5407.
Online: www.citysearch.com/aus/gardenroom.
Accepts: Major credit cards, checks.
Hours: Monday-Saturday 10 a.m. to 5:30 p.m.
Notable: Complete wardrobe consulting.

3 Gardens.

Whether you're planting an herb garden, designing flower beds or sprucing up an existing landscape with benches or fountains, you'll find everything you need here. And add to this comprehensive nursery a shop filled with antique and contemporary furniture, tabletop glassware, amazing textiles, unique food items, European bath treats and books. The

sum is a wonderfully unique mix of merchandise that makes Gardens a shopping experience not to miss. The nursery is lush with live perennials, annuals, succulents and specimen trees, interspersed with water gardens and a beautiful collection of pots. Seeds and bulbs will satisfy those who like to watch things sprout, and an on-site landscape design firm can guide those who have no idea where to start.

To find it: 1818 W. 35th Street, Austin 78703.
Phone: 512/451-5490.
Accepts: MC, Visa, Discover, Amex. Personal checks.
Hours: Monday-Saturday 9 a.m. to 6 p.m. Sunday 11 a.m. to 5 p.m.
Notable: Unique mix of merchandise, from antiques to gourmet foods to all types of plants. Nationally-known landscape design services.

26 **A Good Point.** This spacious and friendly shop bursts with the color of handpainted needlepoint canvas and a rainbow of silks and threads. Brands include Tapestry Tent, Melissa Shirley, Lee Needleart, Strictly Christmas and more.

To find it: 2414 Exposition Blvd. Austin.
Phone: 512/457-8303.
Online: www.agoodpoint.com
Accepts: MC, Visa, Amex. Discover, personal checks.
Hours: Monday-Saturday, 10 a.m. to 5:30 p.m.
Notable: Custom canvas design, including sketches of customers' homes. Toy room to keep children occupied while parents shop.

27 **Feather Your Nest.** Step into this fine linens shop and you'll relax immediately. The soothing, elegant atmosphere is a perfect setting for the luxurious bed and bath linens, sleepwear, and gifts.

Antique silver accents the most beautiful beds in the city, dressed with linens from Sferra Bros., Frette Hotel Collection, Cocoon, Matouk, Leitner, Bella Notte, Pratesi and Palais Royal. Feather beds, down duvets and pillows invite customers to snuggle up. A special Baby's Corner contains the best in linens for the infant room, from blankets and pillows to crib quilts and chenille throws.

If that's not pampering enough, there's sumptuously comfortable night apparel from Hanro and luxurious soaps, bath gels and lotions.

To find it: 2414 Exposition Blvd, A-2.
Phone: 512/476-0187.
Accepts: MC, Visa, Amex. Personal checks.
Hours: Monday-Saturday, 10 a.m. to 5 p.m.
Notable: Fine European linens for bed and bath, plus unique gifts. "Famous" for its gift wrap.

25 **Tarrytown Gallery.** Come in and experience a wide variety of artwork by area artists, including pastels by Dianne Grammer, Glenn Whitehead, Wanda Gamble, and Nancy Bandy; watercolors by Russell BeLue and Kathryn O'Grady; paintings by Roi James, Stella Alesi, and Pablo Taboada. Art consulting and interior design available, as well as complete picture framing services for all media, including photography, needlework, objects. Perfection is a guarantee.

To find it: 2414 Exposition Boulevard, Suite B-110.
Phone: 512/473-2552
Accepts: MC, Visa, Amex, Discover, Personal checks.
Hours: Monday-Friday, 9 a.m. to 5:30 p.m. Saturdays 10 a.m. to 4 p.m.
Notable: Local and regional artists. Complete framing services; French matting a specialty.

West End

W. 12th St.

W. 9th St.

W. Lynn

Tremont Dr.

Highland Ave.

Oakland Ave.

Paul Dressler

Winflo Dr.

Brownlee Cir.

Harthan

Nelson

Blanco

8 th

7th

Baylor S.

Lamar Blvd.

Powell

Sayers

Orchard

4 th

Rose St.

3rd

W. 6th St.

W. 5th St.

N

W   E

S

4 **Zanzibar.** Located in the shade of Treaty Oak, Zanzibar offers stunning handicrafts from tiny, remote villages dotting the globe. Owners Judith and Trey Massengale travel the world searching for treasures to bring back to Austin. "When shoppers walk into our store, I want them to sense the respect we have for the craftsmen and women around the world who don't produce with machines, but with their hands and their souls,"

Judith Massengale says. Zanzibar offers country furniture, exceptional lamps, unusual architectural elements, amazing gifts and contemporary crafts from such locales as the Dutch East Indies, Provincial China, Morocco, Japan, Africa, France and Italy.

To find it: 1009 W. Sixth Street.
Phone: 512/472-9234.
Accepts: Visa/MC. Personal checks.
Hours: Monday-Saturday 10 a.m. to 6 p.m.; Sunday 12-5 p.m.
Notable: Unusual, handcrafted pieces from all over the world.

1 **Durham Trading & Design.** Open this door for a different experience in antiques. Durham Trading & Design's signature style has ventured beyond the typical trappings of a home furnishing store to create a world of vivid juxtapositions: old-world antiques, fine furniture, original art, vintage hunting and fishing collectibles and architectural elements. If you're furnishing your dream house, office, or vacation getaway, step into Durham Trading &

Design and let the experienced interior consultants help you create a stunning look with upholstered furnishings, custom hand-forged iron, or fine Country French pine antiques—or fine American and French antiques. Durham also has an unequaled collection of Texas artisans and architectural antiques. Imagine the statement you can make with carved wooden doors, vintage iron gates, and stained glass windows in your home or office.

To find it: 1009 W. Sixth Street.
Phone: 512/476-1216.
Accepts: Visa/MC/AMEX Personal checks.
Hours: Monday-Saturday 10 a.m. to 6 p.m. Sunday 1-5 p.m.
Notable: Vintage sporting gear, one of Durham's passions. Wonderful eclectic mix allows shoppers to create their own individualized style.

2 Whit Hanks Private Collection.

Whit Hanks is a noted antiques dealer who has earned the designation as Austin's best for ten years running. Nestled among other quality antiques dealers at Whit Hanks Antiques, Whit's own specialty store offers his personal favorites carefully selected in Europe. Country French furniture takes center stage in the store, along with the immensely collectable Herend porcelain—and these pieces are *vintage* dinnerware and giftware. Other fine antiques on display here include English and American pieces. Chandeliers, architectural antiques, and fine accessories round out this special collection.

To find it: 1009 W. Sixth St.
Phone: 512/478-3215
Email: sales@whithanks.com
Online: www.whithanks.com
Accepts: MC, Visa. Personal checks.
Hours: Mon.-Sat., 10 a.m. to 6 p.m.
Notable: Vintage Herend. European antiques handpicked by Austin's leading dealer.

3 Jean-Marc Fray Antiques.

For special, superior-quality antique pieces from France and Italy, visit this extraordinary gallery. Jean-Marc Fray and his wife, Cynthia, are direct importers specializing in the 17th to early 20th centuries.

As a former resident of Nice on the French Riviera, Jean-Marc has a wealth of knowledge in fine French furniture and antique restoration; perhaps that's why this shop is Austin's leading source for unique French furnishings. The Frays make several buying trips to France and Italy each year and will locate specific pieces for clients upon request.

Besides furniture, Jean-Marc Fray houses accessories and art to enhance the look and feel of any home, including original oil paintings and beautiful rugs.

To find it: 1009 W. Sixth St. (at Whit Hanks), Austin, Texas 78703.
Phone: 512/457-0077.
Accepts: MC, Visa. Personal checks.
Hours: Mondays-Saturdays 10 a.m. to 6 p.m. Hours change in Jan. Also open most holidays.
Notable: Exceptional French and Italian antiques. Fine selection of original oils, objets d'art and other decorative arts.

20

11 **Anjely.** When owner Debra Wyka was decorating her home, she was unable to find the quality of African art she wanted. So she decided to open Anjely and sell it herself, along with fine antiques.

The result is a fasinating shop. The African art includes safari animals, hand-painted ostrich eggs from South Africa, Leadwood carvings and Shona Art Sculptures from Zimbabwe, and handcrafted bowls, busts, chess sets, and walking sticks of beautiful Ebony wood from Malawi. One wall is dedicated entirely to African masks and tribal art.

Boxes in different shapes and styles, primitive teak chests, cupboards and trunks are from India, while the antiques include pieces from rustic to Asian to European to American. Notable finds on our visit

included beautiful hunt cupboards and armoires.

To find it: 500 N. Lamar Blvd. Suite 140, Austin, Texas 78703.
Phone: 512/482-0600.
Accepts: MC, Visa, Amex. Personal checks.
Hours: Monday-Saturday 10 a.m. to 6 p.m. except Fridays 10 a.m. to 7 p.m. Sundays 1-5 p.m. Open some holidays.
Notable: Austin's widest selection of African Art. This is *the* place to be for the avid Elephant Collector. Layaway available.

14 **Tipler's Lamp Shop.** Tipler's is the perfect source for quality lighting. They have a large variety of beautiful antique and custom-made table and floor lamps, as well as hanging fixtures and lamp-

shades in a wide selection of materials. Tipler's also handles repair and restoration for all your lighting needs.

To find it: 1204 W. Fifth St., Austin, Texas 78703.
Phone: 512/472-5007
Accepts: MC, Visa. Personal checks.
Hours: Tues.-Sat. 10 a.m. to 5 p.m.

13 **Moss Miciotto.** Austin's finest producer of handcrafted ceramics. The studio offers an ever-changing collection of decorative accessories, ranging from lamps to exceptional gifts.

To find it: 1200B W. Fifth St., Austin, Texas 78703.
Phone: 512/474-9901.
Accepts: MC, Visa.
Hours: Monday-Friday 10 a.m. to 3 p.m. or by appointment.
Online: www.mossmiciotto.com

7 Pecan Square Emporium.

A treat for one and all. Collectibles by Frykman, Lynn Haney, Harmony Kingdom, Charming Tails, Fontanini, Polonaise, Radko and more. Dealer for Snow Village, Heritage Villages and Snowbabies. Authentic German nutcrackers and smoking men by Ulbricht and Steinbach. Designer jewelry, specialty gifts, cards.

To find it: 1122 W. Sixth St.
Phone: 512/477-4900.
Online: www.pecansquare.com.
Accepts: Visa, Amex, MC, Discover. Personal checks.
Hours: Mon.-Sat. 10 a.m. to 6 p.m. Sun. 11 a.m. to 4 p.m. Extended hours, November-December.

6 Fortney's Artful Home Furnishings.

Come inside and wander through a mixture of old and new in an Old Austin atmosphere.

This shop was built as a mom-and-pop grocery in 1927, and it still has the original ceilings and floors. Now, instead of canned goods, flour and sugar, it's stocked with exciting antiques and decorative accessories from all over the world. You'll find furniture and accessories, as well as gifts for discriminating tastes.

To find it: 1116 W. Sixth St.
Phone: 512/495-6505.
Accepts: MC, Visa, Amex Discover. Personal checks.
Hours: Mon.-Sat. 10 a.m. to 6 p.m. Sun. 11 a.m. to 4 p.m.

8 Necessities And Temptations.

Lives up to its name. Austin and Texas souvenirs. T-shirts. Silver, Southwestern jewelry. Frames, candles, vases, chimes, fountains. Rain chime boxes and indoor fountains.

To find it: 1202 W. Sixth St.
Phone: 512/473-8334.
Online: www.necessities.citysearch.com.
Accepts: Visa, MC, Amex, Discover. Personal checks.
Hours: Mon.-Sat. 10 a.m. to 6 p.m. Sun. 11 a.m. to 4 p.m. Extended hours, November-December.

12 **Castle Hill Cafe.** Always ranked among Austin's best restaurants, this comfortable restaurant offers affordable fine food and wine in a warm, eclectic setting.

From a restaurant with just 12 tables, Castle Hill has grown and now includes private dining rooms for special functions. Housed in the former Lindig Grocery, a building constructed in 1897, Castle Hill has retained its original cozy elegance. The feeling is casual, and the rooms are adorned with original art and ceramics by Austin artists Helmut Barnett and Claudia Reese, respectively. Beautiful Oaxacan animal carvings also invite the eye to linger.

But what really makes dining at Castle Hill a treat is the wonderful, creative food. Classified as "New Continental," the menu includes such favorites as lamb empanadas, pad Thai, duck and sausage gumbo, and a mocha toffee torte.

Once you try Castle Hill, you'll want to share it with your colleagues and friends. The private dining rooms are used for corporate and private dinner parties for 25-47 people Mondays-Thursdays. On weekends, they are used to accommodate reservations for groups of six or more.

Whether for a party or a quiet dinner for two, Castle Hill is the perfect venue for a stellar meal. Visit and you'll discover why Austin loves it so much.

To find it: 1101 W. Fifth Street.
Phone: 512/486-0728.
Accepts: Visa, MC, Amex, Discover.
Hours: Lunch served 11 a.m. to 2:30 p.m. Mon.-Fri. Dinner 6-10 p.m. Mon.-Sat. Closes between Christmas and New Year's and the week of July 4.
Notable: Consistently among Austin's favorite fine dining destinations. Private dining rooms available for parties Mondays-Thursdays for up to 47.

5 **Sparks.** Not many shops tolerate customers wielding ice-cream cones, but this neighbor to Amy's Ice Cream says "Come on in!" It's all part of the fun-and-friendly attitude at Sparks, where you can find a card, a gift, jewelry, or a T-shirt. Skagen watches are available here, and the store stocks more than 100 T-shirt styles. Sparks has been named the city's best greeting card shop ('95 and '96), its best source for wrapping paper ('97) and best gift store ('98). Customers really appreciate the wrapping service, which is free as long as you buy the paper and ribbon here; the gifts themselves can be purchased elsewhere. And you will be sure to find a unique greeting card. Sparks specializes in small, alternative and contemporary lines, and handles handmade cards by local artists, too.

To find it: 1014 West Sixth St.
Phone: 512/4-SPARKS (477-2757).
Accepts: Visa, MC, Amex, Discover. Personal checks if in-state.
Hours: Open seven days a week-open late every night.
Notable: Gift-wrapping service even covers gifts bought elsewhere. Represents numerous local artists, with works adorning greeting cards, T-shirts, etc.

10 Twombly Fine Art Consulting.

Dana Twombly delivers the highest level of service to art aficionados looking to start or expand their collections. She performs extensive searches through galleries and individual artists to put together the finest selection of art. Never underestimate the power of art.

To find it: 4712 Ave. H.
Phone: 512/451-0202
Accepts: Personal checks.
Hours: Mon.-Sat. 9 a.m. to 5 p.m.

2 éLan.

Owners Olga Cortez, Michelle Chittim and Mark Evans welcome customers into this comfortable hair and nail salon with great coffee and snacks. Of course, they also offer top-notch cutting, coloring and manicure services as well, to both men and women. After all, the trio has been working in the beauty industry for at least 15 years. Featured products include Alterna, Artec and Brocato.

To find it: 1601 W. 38th St.
Phone: 512/371- é LAN.
Accepts: MC & Visa & Personal checks.
Hours: Tuesday, Wednesday, Friday 9 a.m. to 5 p.m.
Thursday 9 a.m. to 6 p.m.
Saturday 8 a.m. to 2 p.m.
For over 15 years.

9 Wally Workman Gallery.

If you've never been to an art opening at this Sixth Street gallery, then you've never been to an art opening. They are fabulous— almost as fabulous as the art shown in this salon-style gallery. Wally Workman features works by Will Klemm (pictured above), Gordon Fowler and Sarah Higdon, and Linda Dumont, among others; a different artist is showcased in the gallery's main room each month. The gallery's artists have seen their works published by the Winn Art Group and have been recognized by The National Gallery of Art.

When you visit, you will find friendly, knowledgeable sales people to help with your choice. Complete fine-art consultation is available for clients, as well as full-service installation. The gallery also offers museum-quality framing, using only archival materials. Their mouldings include exclusive patterns in fine hardwoods and Texas mesquite.

To find it: 1202 W. Sixth St.
Phone: 512/472-7428.
Accepts: MC, Visa, Amex, Discover. Personal checks.
Hours: Tues.-Sat. 10 a.m. to 5 p.m.
Notable: European, salon-style gallery showcasing contemporary art in a variety of media.

24 **Carpe Diem Salon.** Here on the site of the original Antone's nightclub is this stylish beauty salon. Trust us, the location is their only link to singin' the blues— you'll emerge from Carpe Diem Salon singing a much happier tune! The beautiful atmosphere helps: the building is a beautiful, split level with a glass front, Italian-style arches, stucco walls and colorful artwork. In this warm, comfortable setting, you can receive an array of beauty services, all performed by caring, down-to-earth professionals. Whether you need color or highlights, a hair cut or up-do, or special makeup for a special night on the town, Carpe Diem will deliver. And to bring the salon style home with you, they offer wonderful products. The lines they carry include Tigi, Fudge, Schwarzkopf and Young Living, a boutique, all-natural line that uses 100-percent-pure essential oils.

Address: 115 E. Sixth St., Suite N.
Phone: 512/476-1515.
Accepts: MC, Visa, Amex. Personal checks.
Hours: Tuesday to Friday, 10 a.m. to 7 p.m.; Saturday 9 a.m. to 4 p.m.
Notable: Convenient Sixth Street location across from The Driskill Hotel. Offers cut, color, highlights, up-dos and make-up services.

20 **The Driskill Hotel.** This grande dame of Austin recently got a face lift—and what a face lift it is. The Driskill truly is a grand hotel in the old style, once again. The Driskill originally opened in 1886, and today, following a three-year, $35 million restoration, it has returned to its original, luxurious Victorian splendor.

The Driskill's expert hospitality and opulent surroundings are the perfect backdrop for business meetings and special events as well. The staff delights in hosting one-of-a-kind gatherings, whether intimate dinners in one of the charming private rooms or grand occasions in the majestic ballroom.

To find it: 604 Brazos Street.
Phone: 512/474-5911, 800/252-9367.
Fax: 512/474-2214.
Accepts: All major credit cards.
Hours: 24 hours daily. Check in, 3 p.m. Check out, noon. **The Driskill Grill:** Serving breakfast, lunch, dinner and Sunday brunch. 6:30 a.m. -2 p.m. and 5:30-10 p.m. daily. **Bar:** 11 a.m. to midnight Sunday-Thursday; 11 a.m. to 2 a.m. Friday-Saturday.
Notable: Recently completed $35 million, complete historic restoration. A member of The Leading Hotels of the World, and National Trust Historic Hotels of America. Adjacent to Sixth Street, just blocks from the Texas Capitol and Town Lake.

15 **Crofts Original.** Tucked into historic Clarksville just five minutes from downtown, this charming clothing boutique is not to be missed. Owner Susan Crofts began her new business with a line of handpainted clothing inspired by the Anasazi rock art around Santa Fe. It has naturally evolved as she met other artists and jewelers on her travels. Whenever fun and unusual things crossed her path, Crofts would bring them back to Austin and soon found her customers were also taken with the unique items.

Over the years, Crofts has broadened her selection to include fine clothing and accessories, but she has stuck to her original quest for unusual pieces with their own personality and style. Besides her original line, she has assembled a collection of clothing from designers here and abroad, as well as home accessories and gifts. Now, walking into Crofts Original is a feast for all the senses. Velvets, satins, and cotton provide different textures to touch. Aromatherapy candles add their scent to the air. Treasures are hidden in nooks and crannies all over the store. With such variety, it's easy to find the perfect thing here, whether for yourself or for someone special.

To find it: 1101 W. Lynn. Large parking lot in back of converted house.
Phone: 512/472-4028.
Accepts: Visa, MC. Personal checks with valid ID.
Hours: Monday to Saturday 10 a.m. to 6 p.m.; Sunday 12-5 p.m.
Notable: Handpainted, hand-beaded and hand-embroidered clothing. Gifts Jewelry, cards and home accessories. Everything is original and unique.

19 **Apple Annie's** They opened their doors in 1982 aiming to provide healthy gourmet food to Austin. Eighteen years later, they still are—while catering special events, selling top-notch baked goods all over Texas, and offering corporate gifts galore.

Apple Annie's catering offers creative cuisine for service, including vegetarian selections. From hors d'oeuvres and entrees to sandwiches and salads, these tempting dishes will make your guests rave—even if they're President Clinton and Vice President Gore, who happen to be Apple Annie's clients. Apple Annie's serves businesses, government agencies and individuals, and their expertise can be had either at the café, which is available for afternoon and evening parties, or at the location of your choice.

Apple Annie's also offers box lunches and trays that you can serve yourself, and even gift baskets that you can send to special friends and clients. Whether stuffed with Apple Annie's famous half-pound Volcano Brownies or gourmet cheeses and fruit, the baskets are a welcome treat.

But don't wait until you have a party to taste the food. At Apple Annie's Café Express downtown, you can have breakfast or lunch on weekdays, either inside or outdoors in the open-air courtyard. Feast on homemade salads or sandwiches made on their bakery bread. Hot entrees range from pastas and pizza to grilled chicken, fish and meatloaf. The menu changes daily to make sure all the ingredients are the freshest and best available.

To sample Apple Annie's baked goods, you can visit the café or buy them at many of the city's best grocery stores and restaurants. Apple Annie's is known for its all-natural, preservative-free recipes and its wheat-free spelt products.

To find it: 221 W. Sixth St. in Bank One Tower.
Phone: 512/472-1884.
Accepts: MC, Visa, Amex. Personal checks with proper ID.
Hours: Cafe and Bakery: Monday to Friday 7 a.m. to 2 p.m. Catering seven days a week. Bakery goods available seven days, all over town.
Notable: Catering from box lunches to hors d'oeuvres. Corporate gifts. Downtown café. All-natural baked goods, some wheat-free.

15 Word of Mouth.

Since 1989, Word of Mouth Catering has offered a standard of excellence in custom catering unsurpassed in Central Texas. The company provides the finest seasonal foods prepared and presented with care and artistry from the best quality ingredients, and served by the city's most experienced wait staff.

Don't take our word for it. *Bon Appétit* magazine chose Word of Mouth as one of the ten "Best Wedding Caterers" in the United States. *Austin Chronicle's* critics and its readers have put Word of Mouth on their lists of the Best of Austin, making the company both a Critic's Choice and People's Choice. Meanwhile, the company has been among the 50 fastest-growing privately held concerns in the city for the past three years.

Word of Mouth's event planners work one-on-one with each client to provide the attention to detail needed to create a truly unique event. They are professionals who can assist in every aspect of special events planning, including designing a concept, planning a menu, selecting drinks, handling special equipment, and choosing the decor and entertainment. Whether it is a small, intimate dinner, an important corporate event for thousands, or the wedding reception of a lifetime, Word of Mouth's goal is to exceed your expectations.

To find it: 919 W. 12th Street.
Phone: 512/472-9500.
Accepts: MC, Visa & Checks
Hours: By appointment only.
Notable: Catering service with personal event planners to make every special party a success.

18 El Arroyo.

This local chain of casual Tex-Mex restaurants has been serving up Austin's favorite foods for more than a decade in an atmosphere dubbed "early tacky". Now with three locations and catering service, El Arroyo is never far away when you get a hankering for your favorite tacos, enchiladas and other Mexican specialties.

El Arroyo serves lunch and dinner daily and breakfast on weekends until 3 p.m. For breakfast, try the migas or the tamale omelette, which, according to the menu, sounds great and tastes even better. All breakfast entrees are served with potatoes, napalitos (cactus), and beans.

If you've come in for lunch or dinner, you can't go wrong with the spinach enchiladas or Del Mar enchiladas stuffed with crab and shrimp. Of course, more traditional Mexican entrees are available, from combos like the Federale Special (tamale, enchilada, soft taco, chalupa, rice, beans and a beer) to sizzling fajitas. Or try the barbeque chicken, burgers, or a salad.

El Arroyo Catering brings your favorite menu items to your special event, from an array of appetizers to buffet entrees to dessert. In addition to the food, El Arroyo can provide a margarita, wine and beer bar, and even will arrange for entertainment.

Once you've become an El Arroyo regular, take home a T-shirt or baseball cap to declare your loyalty.

To find it: 1624 W. Fifth, Austin; 301 E. Hwy. 79, Round Rock; 7032 Wood Hollow Drive.

Phone: 512/474-1222 (5th St.), 345-TACO (Far West), 310-1992 (Round Rock).

Accepts: Major credit cards.

Hours: Mon.-Tue., 11 a.m. to 10 p.m.; Wed.-Thu., 11 a.m. to 11 p.m.; Fri., 11 a.m. to midnight; Sat. 10 a.m. to midnight; Sun. 10 a.m. to 10 p.m.

w w w . d i t c h . c o m

23 August Scholz, a German immigrant and confederate veteran, probably did not know how long his name would live in Austin.

Then August Scholz opened Scholz Garten in 1866, and it soon became a favorite meeting place for the area's German population.

As the place grew in popularity, Scholz added the Biergarten and other rooms to accommodate crowds, who turned out for the German food, beer, and atmosphere.

Scholz died in 1891, and then his family sold the establishment to the brewery that produces Falstaff beer. Some 15 years later, a German singing club bought Scholz Garten, and has owned it ever since. The Austin Saengerrunde leases the property to restaurant operators.

Prohibition might have slowed the Garten down, but its savvy managers came up with a non-alcoholic beer and expanded the food menu to include more traditional Texas and regional favorites. Food sales grew quickly and kept things going until alcohol could be sold once again, but stayed strong even then—and today.

Over the years, Scholz Garten has hosted political debates and live music, the former unplanned and the latter by design. In fact, The Garten has attracted quite a few of Austin's up-and-coming musicians, in addition to German bands.

Now, Scholz Garten is the oldest continuously operating business in the state of Texas. It's even older than the present Texas Capitol building. And its old traditions of good food, good music, and cold beer live on.

23 Scholz Garten. In 1966, the Texas Legislature passed a resolution stating that Scholz Garten was "a gathering place for Texans of discernment, taste, culture, erudition," epitomizing the finest tradition of magnificent German heritage in our State.

That was more than thirty years ago, but Scholz Garten still is. In fact, thirty years is just a fraction of the time Scholz Garten has been serving up cold beer, good music, and good food in Austin. Rich in history, Scholz is the last of the "Great Biergartens" in the city. Years ago, it was a place the family could go before "horseless carriages" and "moving pictures" took over the world. At Scholz, the kids could romp around the bandstand, and their parents could enjoy a nice, cold beer. Today, that cold beer and relaxed atmosphere keeps folks coming back. The tradition of hosting up-and-coming Austin musicians, as well as more established bands, helps make its customers loyal. Before and after UT games, it's the hottest spot in town.

To find it: 1607 San Jacinto Blvd.
Phone: 512/474-1958.
Accepts: Major credit cards and personal checks.
Hours: 11 a.m. to 11 p.m. daily.
Notable: Oldest continuously operating business in Texas. Traditional Biergarten. Patio. Live music, good food, cold beer.

Success Stories

Ron & Peggy Weiss Jeffrey Weinberger

A passion for friendship, food and wine was the genesis of this restaurant group. Friends from student days at the University of Texas, Peggy & Ron Weiss and Jeffrey Weinberger pooled their interests, talents, and enthusiasm in 1975 to create Jeffrey's Restaurant and Bar, Austin's first true fine-dining establishment.

Their first foray into the restaurant world became the city's most noted, with the help of Executive Chef David Garrido, and it still looms large on the Austin culinary landscape. But Weiss Weinberger, and company were not satisfied with creating this pearl. Their love of Austin and fine food has led to a strand of dining ventures embodying the best of the city in setting, cuisine, and service.

They dreamed of bringing sophisticated dining to downtown Austin, so ten years ago they opened Shoreline Grill, a comfortable yet elegant restaurant on the bank of Town Lake. Under the leadership of Chef Dan Haverty, Shoreline Grill has won accolades for its food and its spectacular view.

Since then, Ron Weiss has teamed with Jeffrey's executive chef to open Fresh Planet Cafe inside the Whole Foods Market flagship store. The original group then created Cipollina, a neighborhood cafe, gourmet shop and take-out spot in the Clarksville neighborhood near Jeffrey's.

So when Austinites savor Garrido's black bean ravioli with duck and shrimp in a black truffle sherry cream sauce or Haverty's beef tenderloin with ancho cajeta sauce, they have this trio of friends to thank for the experience. Without them, Austin's food culture would not be so tasty.

17 Jeffrey's.

If Austin has a culinary landmark, this is it. Jeffrey's was Austin's first upscale dining spot, and many say it's still the best. Executive Chef David Garrido's pitch-perfect palate has yielded a culinary style exclusively his: a masterful blend of Southwest and Latin tastes with continental technique. The result is vivid, sophisticated food that lingers in the memory and pairs beautifully with wine. Add the restaurant's warm, friendly service and a *Wine Spectator*-lauded wine list, and you have the most well-rounded dining experience in the city. No wonder Austinites select it as the city's best restaurant year after year.

To find it: 1204 W. Lynn Street.
Phone: 512/477-5584.
Accepts: Major credit cards.
Hours: Monday-Thursday from 6 p.m. Friday-Sunday from 5:30 p.m.
Notable: Two dining rooms for private functions. Noted chef. Award-winning wine list. Consistently voted Austin's best restaurant.

16 Cipollina.

In bringing Italian back to the Clarksville neighborhood, Cipollina became a culinary chameleon. It's a neighborhood cafe. Created by the owners of Jeffery's, it is an Italian rosticceria, where take-out is an art form. An authentic Italian pantry. So whether you want a pastry and cappucino in the morning, a wood-fired pizza or pasta salad at noon, or a take-home dinner of osso buco and polenta for family and friends, Cipollina can provide it. You can even stop by to stock up on the finest olive oils, vinegars, caviar and foie gras. In sum, you can eat well, save time, de-stress and improve your culinary reputation.

To find it: 1213 W. Lynn Street.
Phone: 512/477-5211.
Accepts: Major credit cards.
Hours: Daily 7:30 a.m. to 8 p.m.
Notable: Artful take-out Italian food for family or dinner parties. Casual breakfasts and lunches. Fine pantry provisions.

14 **Austin Land & Cattle Company.** Step into this casually elegant steakhouse and enjoy sophisticated steak, poultry and seafood by candlelight. They've won accolades here for their beef, hand-cut here at the restaurant. Whether your pleasure is Ribeye, Filet Mignon, a New York Strip or

Top Sirloin, you'll find satisfaction in these tender specimens. There's pork chops and chicken breast for white-meat eaters and even a portobello mushroom steak as a vegetarian option. Or try the innovative seafood: peppercorn-encrusted yellowfin tuna, South American lobster tail and more. Of course there are soups, salads and sides, not to mention dessert, all served up by the friendly, knowledgeable staff. Have a drink from the full bar or a selection from the extensive wine list to round out your meal.

To find it: 1205 N. Lamar Boulevard.
Phone: 512/472-1813.
Accepts: All major credit cards.
Hours: Sunday-Thursday 5-10 p.m.;
Friday-Saturday 5-11p.m.
Notable: Award-winning aged steaks hand-cut on the premises. Fresh, innovative seafood. Voted best steak in town. Three stars from the *Austin American-Statesman*.

16 **The Tavern.** Located in an old grocery story modeled after a German public house, this hangout has a rich history. During the Depression, the best steaks in town were served up here for 50 cents, and during Prohibition, the upstairs quarters were a rumored speakeasy and red-light hotel. (The spirit of that era lives on with the resident ghost, Emily, who creaks the upstairs floorboards and likes the sound of breaking glass.) Popular post-Prohibition with legislators, soldiers and the growing citizenry—not to mention the Longhorns, who still call it their own—The Tavern escaped the wrecking ball when Lamar was paved. Today, it remains a meeting place, a sports bar with more than a dozen televisions and satellite sports, a student hangout. Ice-cold beer and home-cooked meals keep 'em coming back, and don't miss all those stories carved into the bar. As they say around here, you're never too far from 12th and Lamar.

To find it: 12th St. and Lamar Blvd.
Phone: 512/474-7496.
Accepts: Major credit cards.
Hours: 11 a.m. to 2 a.m. daily.
Notable: Happy Hour weekdays 3-7 p.m. Daily Lunch specials. Coldest beer in Austin. Sports bar with 13 televisions and satellite programming.

22 Shoreline Grill. The team behind Austin's dining superstar, Jeffrey's restaurant, brings sophisticated, eclectic dining to downtown Austin with this eatery overlooking Town Lake. From business power lunches to distinctive dinners, Shoreline Grill offers meals that reflect their origins in fresh, quality ingredients, in an atmosphere of comfortable elegance. It doesn't hurt that the dining room and balcony offer stunning views of the lake and the restaurant's famous neighbor, the Congress Avenue Bat Colony, which wheels into the sky in the summer sunset. Desserts are as delectable as the scenery—try the famous Chocolate Intemperance.

To find it: 98 San Jacinto Blvd.
Phone: 512/477-3300 for reservations; 477-7598 for private events.
Fax: 512/477-6392
Accepts: Major credit cards.
Hours: Lunch Mondays-Fridays from 11:00 a.m.; dinner nightly from 5:00 p.m.
Notable: View of Town Lake, Congress Avenue bats. Private parties for 20-50 people or events for up to 400.

17 Crystal Works. Owner Cathleen Day-Woodruff started her crystal business in 1977 with a box of leaded crystal that she sold at craft fairs. Fourteen years ago, she opened her first store inside Book People. Now, she has her own place, which she runs with the help of her children, Hanna, Daniel, and Sam. The name of this shop only hints of the riches inside. Of course Crystal Works carries crystals, both leaded and natural. But Crystal Works also boasts a collection of Feng Shui supplies, fountains, mineral specimens, seashell boxes, fossils, books and more for the home. Plus, there's 14-karat gold jewelry and sterling silver rings. So come in to adorn your body and your home.

To find it: 908A West 12th Street, Austin, Texas 78703. At 12th and Lamar behind The Tavern, Bookwoman and Austin Artisans.
Phone: 512/472-5597.
Accepts: MC, Visa, Amex, Discover. Personal checks.
Hours: Monday to Thursday 10 a.m. to 9 p.m.; Friday and Saturday 10 a.m. to 10 p.m.; Sunday 11 a.m. to 7 p.m.

35

ATTRACTIONS:
The Bat Colony

Leave it to Austin to make a mistake into a tourist attraction.

Almost 20 years ago, bridge engineers designed repairs to the Congress Avenue bridge that, unbeknownst to them, would make it nirvana for bat mothers-to-be. The bridge's new expansion joints became crevices crying out for bats to take roost and multiply.

And take roost they did. Within five years, so many bats had congregated under the bridge that Austin had the world's largest urban bat colony.

That's not to say that Austin was proud—at least not at the time. The local citizenry shunned the small airborne creatures. But conservationists pointed out that bats consume up to 30,000 insects nightly, including mosquitoes and agricultural pests, lessening the need for chemical pesticides. Well, Austin has never been deaf to an environmental appeal. Efforts to eradicate the "pests" screeched to a halt, and viola! A tourist attraction was born.

From the time the Mexican freetail bats arrive in the spring until they leave for points south on the tailwinds of the first cold fronts, they emerge each night in a wheeling ballet of black against the evening sky. Tourists and locals gather on both banks of Town Lake or on the bridge

itself to gape at the sight. Meanwhile, the mostly female bats give birth and nurse their young in the bridge's crevices, in preparation for the fall migration.

More information on the bat colony can be found at a kiosk at the *Austin American-Statesman's* observation center, a grassy knoll on the south shore of the lake. For directions, log on to the newspaper's web site, www.austin360.com and search for "bats". Another information kiosk sits before the Four Seasons Hotel, on the lake's north side.

August is the best time to view the bats, because the babies are mature enough to fly with their mothers. But the bats can be seen anytime from mid-March through October.

They come out around sunset.

To find out what time they're likely to emerge each night, call Bat Conservation International, a nationwide leader in bat conservation and education, based in Austin. Their hotline can be reached at 512/416-5700; select category 3636.

BCI has advocated for protective legislation and has cooperated with governments to secure significant bat colonies nationwide. They also educate people about bats and their benefits to the environment. Members of the organization receive a magazine, BATS, and have opportunities to participate in eco tours and workshops. For more information, call 512/327-9721 or visit BCI's web site at 222. batcon.org.

13 Dreyfus Antiques Brocante.

This shop is hard to miss, given the owner's little bit of "home" out front—an exact replica of the Eiffel Tower. This landmark reflects owner George Dreyfus' heritage; the first family antique store was established in Paris in 1875. Following his great-grandparents' tradition, Dreyfus opened this store in 1990. Its spacious showroom contains an exceptional collection of country French antiques.

To procure his merchandise, Dreyfus travels from Bordeaux to Aix-en-Provence, with a short stop in Paris for "Aux Prues"—the city's biggest and most important antique market. The store offers a unique selection of 18th- and 19th-century armoires, tables, hutches, chairs, tapestries, architectural pieces and decorative items. Interspersed among these, you will also find garden accessories such as striking Provencal jars and classic iron gates and fences.

To find it: 1901 N. Lamar at MLK Blvd.
Phone: 512/473-2443.
Accepts: MC/VISA/AMEX Personal checks.
Hours: Monday-Saturday 10 a.m. to 7 p.m.; Sunday 1-5 p.m.
Notable: Country French furniture, garden pieces, decorative accessories.

11 The Flower Bucket.

A full-service florist with the atmosphere of a European flower market, The Flower Bucket has an impressive array of artistically designed arrangements of blooming and green plants. Come and select one to take home, or have one delivered to a friend. When you're planning a special event, the floral designers here can arrange their wares in lavish displays or understated simplicity to enhance your wedding, reception, or party. And when you stop by, browse through the extraordinary selection of collectibles. From luxurious soaps and lotions to Latin American folk art and decorative garden accessories, you are sure to find something for that special someone.

To find it: 3100 N. Lamar.
Phone: 512/453-6692.
Accepts: All major credit cards. Personal checks. In-house credit accounts available.
Hours: Monday-Friday 8 a.m. to 6 p.m.; Saturday 9 a.m. to 6 p.m.
Notable: Wonderful collection of gifts. Fresh flowers and plants shipped in daily. Their talented floral designers can give any special event a special flair.

12   Anne Kelso Day Spa.

Anne Kelso is a full service hair and body salon offering an entire complement of beauty services. Your relationship with Anne Kelso may begin with an update to

the already fabulous you, and then evolve into a complete revival of your essential well-being. From traditional facials, manicures and pedicures to innovative body wraps and rubs, the salon's services are designed to make the most of the time that **you have for you.** When time does allow, sample the extraordinary with a Spa Manicure/Pedicure, European facial and Healing massage.

To find it: 3018 N. Lamar Blvd.
Phone: 512/467-2663.
www.annekelso@citysearch.com
Accepts: Major credits cards, personal checks.
Hours: Monday 10 a.m. to 4 p.m.
Tuesday-Friday 9 a.m. to 7 p.m.
Saturday 9 a.m. to 5 p.m.
Notable: In-house and out-call services for basic and customized treatments, designed to meet each client's individual needs.

18 Whole Foods Market.

One store at 9th Street and Lamar has grown into a chain of monuments to the natural lifestyle. (See Success Story, Page 66) Now, Whole Foods Markets—whichever one you choose—are meccas for those seeking easy access to organic, healthy, and environmentally friendly foods and related products.

But although Whole Foods is serious about its products, shopping here is relaxed and fun. Tastings are common, especially on weekends, and a team-oriented management style makes for a friendly, knowledgeable, and helpful staff who'll often go out of their way to make sure customers get what they need.

Whole Foods combines the best attributes of an old-fashioned, neighborhood grocery store, an organic farmer's market, a European bakery, a New York Deli, and a supermarket. Much of the produce is bought from local farmers practicing organic cultivation. The house bakery turns out a wide range of goods every day, from muffins and artisan breads to offerings for vegans and those on wheat-free diets. Bulk coffee, flours and grains, dried fruits and pastas make it simple to stock up on staples. Plus, Whole Foods stocks vitamins and other supplements, natural beauty and body care products, bulk herbs and spices, and lots more. It's truly one-stop shopping.

To find it: Downtown: 601 N. Lamar, Suite 100. **Gateway:** 9607 Research Blvd., Suite 300.
Phone: Downtown: 512/476-1206. **Gateway:** 512/345-5003.
Accepts: Visa, MC, Amex, Discover. Personal checks with proper ID.
Hours: Downtown: 8 a.m. to 10 p.m. daily. **Gateway:** 8 a.m. to 10:30 p.m. daily.
Notable: Homegrown chain retailer of natural, organic and environmentally friendly foods. Huge selection, including house brand. Extensive deli and take-out.

18 Fresh Planet Cafe.

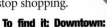

Located inside the flagship Whole Foods Market, this restaurant serves up fresh cuisine in a warm, casual atmosphere. Bright colors and dark wood accents create a friendly place for a quick snack or pleasurable meal. Designed by the executive chef of Jeffrey's, David Garrido, the menu offers up Asian and Mexican specialties built with fresh ingredients. Sandwiches, salads, entrees, wraps and smoothies all are available via counter service for eat-in or take-out.

To find it: 601 N. Lamar, Suite 200.
Phone: 512/476-0902.
Accepts: All major credit cards, personal checks.
Hours: Mon.-Sat. 11 a.m. to 9 p.m.; Sun. 9 a.m. to 6 p.m.

www.granitehouse.com

GRANITE HOUSE

10 Dwight Adair has seen the future, and the future is content.

No, not content, as in happy to be alive. Content, as in table of contents. Stories. Specifically, stories told in pictures: feature films, television series and specials, and corporate video.

Adair knows that if network television, cable channels, and the Internet are screaming for good "content" now, their screams will grow louder as technology provides more places to broadcast their offerings.

So when Adair says he and his two partners at Granite House—a producer of full-service films, videos and multimedia—are in the business of creating content, he means that they're on the express train to the future of the film industry. And he's taking Austin along with him.

Since Adair and his wife, Sandra, a sought-after film editor, came back to Texas in 1993 after almost two decades in the thick of Hollywood, they have tried to help foster the city's already-growing film industry. Just being here helps, because the more film-related talent available locally, the easier it is for producers to staff up. But Adair also has rolled up his sleeves and promoted Austin as a filmmaker's destination.

His business activities have helped boost the industry, too. Adair runs Granite House with cinematographer Mike Martin and Lucy Frost, a high-tech marketing maverick. With their three diverse backgrounds, Granite House takes on a broad variety of projects, from corporate videos for such clients as Dell Computer Corp. and The University of Texas to the feature films and television series that they now are developing. The three partners also use their expertise to help others in the business launch their own projects.

"We want to see our industry grow and we are doing our best to be on the cutting edge of that growth."

Central Park. This mixed-use development, a partnership between the state, the City of Austin, and its developer, features an 11-acre retail center set among three beautiful xeriscaped water quality ponds, a one-quarter-mile jogging track, and picnic areas under more than 40 historic oaks.

During construction, meticulous attention was paid to preserving the tranquility of the area. The climbing roses that ring the property were carefully removed and nurtured during construction, and then returned to their original locations. It's now possible to stop and smell these very roses while you're shopping a mix of eclectic, Austin-owned stores, including those listed on the next three pages.

To find it: 4001 N. Lamar Blvd.
Accepts: Varies by store.
Hours: Vary by store.
Notable: Unique gifts, handmade pottery and jewelry, clothing, and more. Beautiful, nature-oriented setting.

5 WalkTex. Owners Paul and Sheila Carrozza have seen a flurry of non-runners visit their RunTex stores and buy running shoes. Because there is a huge difference between running and walking footwear, they decided to open a walking-specific shoe store. WalkTex carries dozens of styles and sizes, along with a large assortment of walking apparel, accessories, and nutritional supplements. The knowledgeable staff can help you choose the best shoe and apparel for you.

To find it: 4001 N. Lamar Blvd.
Phone: 512/454-9255.
Online: www.runtex.com offers info on events, including walking-oriented races.
Accepts: Major credit cards; personal, local checks with proper ID.
Hours: 10 a.m. to 6 p.m. Monday-Saturday; 1-4 p.m. Sunday.

7 Central Market. Here's a store for people who love to eat, and if they like to cook, too—well, so much the better. It's a gourmand's delight, from the 500 varieties of produce to 2,000 labels of wine. The fresh fish and seafood department boasts the best selection west of the Mississippi, and the meat and poultry cases show off the best variety in town. The European-style bakery is a yeasty-smelling heaven of more than 60 different bread varieties, and an in-house tortilleria produces a a variety of special creations. Or how about the Pastry shop, with its incomparable variety of sweet treats? In the deli, you can find genuine Italian prosciutto, smoked salmon, pate, and more. If you're a cheese lover, there's no better place to find that special variety. And the specialty foods aisles are stocked with more than 13,000 products from around the world, to complete the most basic or most exotic dish.

Don't feel like cooking? Stop by Cafe on the Run, where you'll find chef-prepared salads and sandwiches, as well as main-and side-dish fare to take home. Or relax at the Central Market Cafe, which showcases the best of the store's fresh ingredients.

To find it: 4001 N. Lamar Blvd. in Central Park; 4477 S. Lamar Blvd. at Ben White.
Phone: 512/206-1000 north, 899-4300 south.
Accepts: MC, Visa, Discover, Amex, debit cards. Personal checks.
Hours: Central Park Store: 9 a.m. to 9 p.m. daily. **Cafe:** 7 a.m. to 10 p.m. daily.
Notable: Gargantuan selection of all foodstuffs, from produce and meats to seafood and wine. Specialty products from around the world. In-house baked goods. Cooking school.

6 Scarbroughs at Central Park.

If it's happening in the world of fashion, it's sure to be showcased here at Scarbroughs.

If you want the latest, greatest fashion looks, check out the clothing and accessories at this totally Austin, upscale specialty store for women. Choose a great pair of cheetah capris, dazzling silver mules, colorful silk ball skirts, or the prettiest power bead bundles you've ever seen.

Scarbroughs also addresses the dynamic fashion needs of Austin's pinstripe professionals—and the city's soccer moms—Scarbroughs features beautiful, modern classics such as St. John Knits, Garfield & Marks suits, and Barry Bricken sportswear. A staff of friendly, fashion-savvy associates suggests creative, eclectic looks and ideas that will entice even the most reticent shoppers.

Did we mention the fun, really fun accessories? If it's a hot accessory trend, this store has it and then some. The endless varieties of affordable accessories set Scarbroughs apart. Selections in jewelry, handbags, belts, sunglasses and scarves add polish and pizzazz to a unique apparel selections.

Scarbroughs also offers quality cosmetics from Estee Lauder and Lancome, and features leisurely makeovers by hip makeup artists.

This store aims to please. With a focus on personal service, associates frequently schedule off-hours appointments for harried customers, and they delight in securing special orders. The store offers beautiful, complimentary pre-wrap and charges only token fees for expert alteration service.

The store's light-hearted, fun ambience keeps the ever-growing group of diverse regulars coming back for more. Come see for yourself and feel the energy at Scarbroughs!

To find it: 4001 N. Lamar Blvd. in Central Park.
Phone: 512/452-6026.
Accepts: All major credit cards.
Hours: Mondy-Saturday 10-6 p.m., Thursday 10-8 p.m., Sunday 12-5 p.m.
Notable: Exciting up to the minute fashions.

43

8 Clarksville Pottery & Galleries.

Founded more than 20 years ago as a small pottery studio in the historic Austin neighborhood of Clarksville, Clarksville Pottery & Galleries has grown to become one of the top American craft galleries in the nation.

The gallery's new owners, Connie and Tom Quilter, are enthusiastic about preserving its reputation and continuing its traditions. As Austin has come to expect from Clarksville Pottery, the Quilters present an exciting and ever-changing portfolio of creative artistry from regional and national artisans. For them, just as for the gallery's founders in the 1970s, the retailing of unique, handmade craft art represents a mid-life career change—and a dream come true. Connie and Tom draw upon their years of experience in collecting fine crafts and maintaining relationships with artists nationally.

Clarksville is truly a feast for the eyes and an inspiration for the soul. Among the many treasures you'll find here are contemporary jewelry, a dazzling wedding ring collection named "Best of Austin", and an incomparable assortment of perfectly crafted jewelry boxes. Clarksville's heritage, of course, lies in hand-thrown pottery, and you'll find exquisite examples in brightly colored hues, from raku-fired decorative vessels to functional pieces for everyday use. And the artistry here extends to whimsical leather animals; garden sprinklers and water fountains; museum-quality hand-blown art glass; one-of-a-kind interior accents and furnishings; and richly colorful abstract wall art.

Because all of the work here is handmade fine craft from America, Clarksville's knowledgeable sales staff serve as a valuable link between the customer and the artist. Many custom orders are arranged to meet the customer's unique needs. A special treat is gift-wrapping with Clarksville's exclusive hand-painted paper, each package an original work of art. Austinites have come to recognize a Clarksville package—and to anticipate the wonderful treasure inside.

To find it: 4001 N. Lamar Blvd. Suite 200, in Central Park, next to Central Market.
Phone: 512/454-9079.
Accepts: Visa, MC, Amex, Discover. Personal checks with proper ID.
Hours: Monday to Saturday 10 a.m. to 6:30 p.m., except open until 8 p.m. Thursday; Sunday 12-6 p.m.
Notable: Nationally known gallery of fine American craft. Hand-painted gift wrap.

21 **Lone Star Internet.** Lone Star Internet, Inc. You want to take advantage of all the internet has to offer, but can't get the a straight answer about what it takes?

Join the club.

So many companies know they want to take advantage of the Internet and e-commerce, but that's where their knowledge ends. Enter Lone Star Internet, Inc., a company that not only can design your website and integrate e-commerce into your current systems - it can help you dovelope a complete internet marketing strategy. Lone Star's forte lies in educating its clients about the Internet and how to best capitalize on the opportunities it offers.

For example. Lone Star makes sure that client's web sites contain the information web surfers are seeking. "Consumers will flock to a site that provides factual information about how to make an educated purchasing decision. A simple online brochure just won't generate business," says owner Ken Biggs.

Indeed, many people go online just to get information on products and services in a "non-confrontational environment," Biggs notes. An effective web site does not just advertise prices and availability, but it also anticipates customers' questions and provides them with answers.

Lone Star's job begins with a series of getting-to-know-you sessions. The company finds out about each client's goals and objectives so that a comprehensive marketing strategy can be formulated. "We review how business generated by the web site will be serviced by your company, and determine what level of commitment will be required to manage an effective web site strategy, before we ever discuss what the site will look like," Biggs explains.

Once the site is designed, Lone Star helps businesses expand by integrating e-commerce into the order processing, inventory tracking, shipping and other existing systems of a company. Lone Star a leader in technology allowing clients to update their own web sites frequently with little or no knowledge of programming also allows clients to keep the information on their site fresh and changing to attract visitors again and again.

And to make sure that the visitors to your site want to return, Lone Star makes sure download speed is optimized. They closely monitor their bandwidth and keep plenty of additional capacity available to make sure that heavy traffic doesn't slow any site down.

Have questions about what to do on the Internet? Call Lone Star Internet, Inc. to get the information you need to make an educated decision. Or visit Lone Star's web site (listed below) to find out more.

Lone Star's web site provides a wealth of Texas information for visitors and residents alike. The Guide To Texas Outside at www.texasoutside.com (also developed by Lone Star) is a great place to find outdoor activities in the Austin area as well as the entire state of Texas.

To find it: 800 Brazos, Suite 220, Austin, Texas 78701.
Phone: 512/708-8006, 800/538-0538.
Fax: 512/708-8044.
Website: www.lone-star.net.
Email: biz@lone-star.net.

45

Texas should thank its lucky lone star for James A. Michener, who gave $19 million to endow a Master of Fine Arts program in creative writing at the University of Texas. This interdisciplinary program requires students to work in at least two genres—fiction, screenwriting, poetry and playwriting—and actually pays students $15,000 a year to spend their time writing. Michener's idea was to train professional writers, not writers who must teach to earn a living, so he felt they should learn more than one kind of writing. He also believed that writing students should spend their hours plying their craft, rather than worrying about paying the bills.

Perhaps that's why so many of the Michener Center's graduates go on to see their plays and screenplays produced; publish novels and short-story collections; and win major awards. Its growing reputation has attracted visiting faculty such as Denis Johnson, James Kelman and J.M. Coetzee.

An annual reading series puts the James A. Michener Center for Writers in the spotlight. Every year, the series attracts the likes of Michael Ondaatje, Tim O'Brien and Thom Jones in fiction; Louise Glück and W.S. Merwin in poetry; playwright Tom Stoppard; and Lawren Kasdan and Paul Schrader in screen-

writing.

The permanent faculty also is impressive, led by novelist James Magnuson, who also has produced a number of works for the screen. Magnuson (pictured above left with 1998 graduate David Cleaves, the late Michener, and 1997 graduate Steve Blackburn) has been director of the center since 1994. His most recent novel, *Windfall*, appeared in early 1999. Austin's screenwriter and novelist Stephen Harrigan, whose novel, *The Gates of the Alamo*, appearing in February, also teaches for the Center.

Michener graduates themselves have produced too many works to mention. If their writing credits are a measure of the center's success, then Michener's generosity was well founded.

Texas State House in Strong Sunset
By Linda Dumont

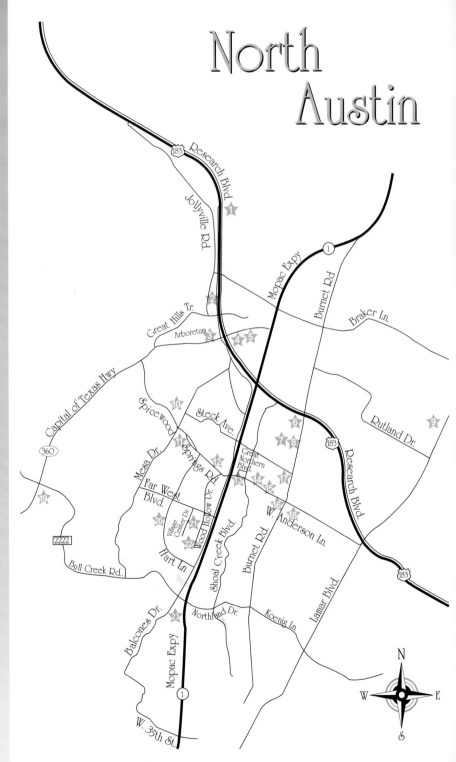

North Austin

North Austin houses the city's future. Many of the high-tech companies that fuel Austin's economy either migrated or grew up here, including the city's corporate giant, Dell Computer Corp. The high-tech pedigree lends this region of the city a fast, slick pace. Like the technology its businesses create, much of the development here is new—new roads, new shopping centers, new office buildings, new homes. But you can find nature if you like in one of the area's nature preserves and parks. The Forest Ridge Nature Preserve even nurtures the rare golden-cheeked warbler.

Baylor University Executive MBA Program.

Todayís marketplace requires that executives and managers cultivate an awareness of evolving economic, technological, and political forces as well as understand the relationships among organizational structures, cultures, and systems.

The goal of executive education at Baylor is to assist working professionals who want to broaden their business expertise and analytical skills while still employed full time.

Baylor University offers Executive MBA programs in Dallas and on the Baylor campus in Waco and Executive Education Seminars to meet the development needs of business professionals.

Additionally, the EMBA programs are enhanced by providing students access to the latest in technological resources and exposure to global business practices. Baylorís executive education programs draw upon Hankamerís recognized strengths as a professional school and collect the broad expertise of its faculty as consultants to business and as recognized scholars for their discovery-oriented research.

The 22-month curriculum combines theory and practical application and examines managerial issues such as globalization, strategic alliances, and technology management in both traditional and energy industries. For advancing managers, the EMBA offers an extraordinary opportunity to acquire one of the best and most comprehensive management educations available.

To find it: P.O. Box 98013, Waco, Texas 76798. Austin office opening soon.
Phone: 254/710-3622, 800/583-3622.
Fax: 254/710-1066.
Online: http://hsb.baylor.edu/EMBA.
Notable: One of America's "Most-Wired Colleges." Residence weeks interspersed with evening classes in Waco and alternating weekends in Dallas and Web-based interaction. Third residence week overseas, destination determined by students.

8 Desert Moon.

Beautiful, Southwestern furniture designed just for you. A dream? No. Thanks to James Robertson, who created Desert Moon in 1976, you can have unique furniture that is custom-made to Robertson's designs and your specifications from kiln-dried hardwoods. A design consultant can visit your home to take measurements, coordinate colors and discuss features you want to include. You select the upholstery, stain and tile patterns. Desert Moon does the rest.

To find it: Visit our showroom, at 8023-B Burnet Road.
Phone: 512/452-3920
512/452-3875.
Accepts: MC, Visa, Discover. Personal checks.
Hours: Monday to Saturday 10 a.m. to 6 p.m.; Sunday 12-5 p.m.
Notable: Each piece is one-of-a-kind. All are designed with customer's input. Lifetime warranty.

7 AquaTek Tropical Fish.

Almost 20 years of keeping aquariums, first as a hobbyist and now a professional, gives Roger Vitko a special perspective when it comes to selling fish and supplies. He's an expert—and a perfectionist.

His goal: To use the scientific method and modern technology to achieve a near-zero loss rate. Which means that, if you're the average aquarium-keeper, you need his help.

But even if you're an expert yourself, AquaTek has something for you. Seven thousand gallons of freshwater aquariums and 1,200 gallons in saltwater ensure that there's plenty to browse through. Vitko's selection of species includes all the common ones, but a good many rare ones as well. His collection of premium aquarium products, including the German brands Tunze and Eheim & Knop, offers customers excellent value for their long life, reduced maintenance and availability of parts for repair.

To find it: 8023 Burnet Road.
Phone: 512/450-0182.
Accepts: MC, Visa, Amex, Discover, Diners, Carte Blanche, ATM. Personal checks.
Hours: Monday to Thursday, 10 a.m. to 8 p.m.; Friday 10 a.m. to 10 p.m.; Saturday 10 a.m. to 8 p.m.; Sunday 12-8 p.m.
Notable: Wide selection, including rare species. High-tech products improve fish survival. Handles aquarium repairs.

18 **Scrapbook Cupboard.**
Slipping your photographs into a photo album? That's passé. These days, scrapbooking is the way to go, and here you'll find everything you need to make a one-of-a-kind memory album—including the experts to teach you how!

Scrapbook Cupboard has thousands of supplies to make your scrapbook pages unique, from background papers in hundreds of styles to stencils to stickers to patterned scissors. But this is much more than a store. It's a workshop, complete with a power punch, die-cut machine, templates and other supplies available for customers' use. It's a party spot, where scrapbook hounds gather to create pages and swap ideas. It's a scrapbooking school, where neophytes can learn the basics and experts can refine their techniques during regularly scheduled classes. And it's a scrapbook atelier. Bring your shoebox of photos, and the staff will create a scrapbook just for you.

To find it: 2165 W. Anderson Lane in the North Star Home Center.
Phone: 512/420-0077.
Accepts: MC, Visa. Personal checks.
Hours: Monday to Saturday, 10 a.m. to 6 p.m.; Thursday 10-8. Late hours on class nights; call ahead to confirm.
Notable: Great selection, including supplies from small, specialty makers. Classes, parties, one-on-one coaching. Custom scrapbook design.

Personal Chef Service
It's All About Thyme

You realized long ago that you're too busy to cook. But you're tired of scanning restaurant menus, sick of take-out containers, and weary of frozen dinners.

Not to worry. Personal Chef Claudia Gerardo can come to the rescue.

With one phone call, you can set up a regular schedule of home-cooked meals, prepared in your kitchen of the freshest ingredients available, including fresh herbs.

Chef Claudia will interview you about your family's tastes and dietary requirements. She'll ask for any favorite recipes. And then she will concoct a two-week set of entrees and sides for your approval. The chef has a repertoire of more than 300 entrees, so you won't see the same meal twice within six months—unless you request a repeat of one of your favorites.

Then she puts on her toque and goes to the market— or two or three, if necessary. Chef Claudia buys only the freshest vegetables, fruits, fish and meats available, even if she has to drive all over town to buy her ingredients!

Finally, she comes to your kitchen, laden with good things and all the utensils she needs to complete your meals. When she's finished, your kitchen is spotless, and your freezer is full of carefully packaged meals, complete with thawing and reheating instructions, and tonight's dinner is waiting for you to do the final cooking.

"By following these instructions, your meals will taste like they were just prepared," Chef Claudia says.

Phone: 512/263-8456.
Notable: Personal chef using freshest ingredients. Can cook to special dietary requirements.

23 Chez Zee.

As Austin's only art cafe and dessert bakery, Chez Zee holds a special place in the pantheon of restaurants here. The eclectic menu and festive atmostphere make any meal seem like a celebration, especially when you make dessert the big finale.

Owners Patrick Dixson and Sharon Watkins are generous with care and attention for their guests. Patrick's milieu is the kitchen, where he collaborates with the chefs to create Chez Zee's wonderful menu. His experience with the Brennan family restaurants in New Orleans help him craft recipes that meld French, Cajun, and Southern sensibilities. Meanwhile, Sharon is responsible for the creative ambience that makes Chez Zee so unique. She displays her own art collection here, and her pieces illustrate her credentials as a longtime art collector and City of Austin arts commissioner. Folk art from Mexico, Spain, and the Caribbean mix with contemporary art on these walls to hold diners' interest. Local artists also display their work, as Chez Zee does its part to nurture the Austin art scene. In fact, the Austin Chronicle has voted the restaurant as Best Springboard for Local Artists. A lovely covered outdoor patio, professionally landscaped with native and other plants, completes the picture.

Patrick's kitchen expertise and Sharon's front-of-the-house panache make for a one-of-a-kind combination. Chez Zee's casual elegance make it perfect for a business lunch or a special meal. Stop by anytime for an espresso and a treat from the bakery, or appetizers and drinks. Try the Crabmeat Quesadillas with Raspberry Salsa or the Roasted Corn and Crab Cakes with Fiery Apple Chutney with your apertif—they'll wet your appetite for more of Chez Zee's great food.

House specialties include Mediterranean Pasta, Tequila Lime Chicken Grille, Jalapeno Cornbread stuffed chicken breast and a Pecan-Crusted Chicken Caesar. Breakfast and and brunch dishes are also standouts; try the Creme Brulee French Toast made from challah and creme brulee and topped with fresh berries, or the succulent, savory migas.

We hope you've saved room for dessert, because Chez Zee's are the best in town. The in-house pastry chef offers ecstasy on a plate. Chocaholics will love the imaginative and rich Chocolate Decadence Cake, and cheesecake aficionados will delight in the selection of flavors (how about Raspberry Truffle?). Kahlua Crunch Pie, Coconut Cream Pie, and Key Lime Pie are just three of the varieties to please pie-lovers. Add Italian Cream Cake, Maida's Cake and other layered delights, and you'll know why Chez Zee is consistently chosen as the best place in Austin to enjoy dessert.

After such an enjoyable experience, you'll leave Chez Zee reluctantly. But don't worry—you can always come back for more!

To find it: 5406 Balcones.
Phone: 512/454-2666.
Accepts: Major credit cards.
Hours: M-Thurs 11 a.m.-10:30 p.m.
Fri-Sat. 9 a.m.-Midnight.
Sun. 9-3-Brunch 3-10 p.m. grille/dinner
Private dinners small banquets.
Rehearsal dinners up to 50.
Cocktail or Desert Parties.
Notables: Baby grand piano, 20 desserts, cookies, made by our party chef. Full bar. Wines by the glass. Reservations taken for all times.

© JAMES INNES

20 Austin Jewish Community Center.

WIth the help of Michael Dell, Austin now has a Jewish Community Center, complete with a state-of-the-art fitness center, park, day care, and special-events facilities.

On a 40-acre site, the Jewish Community Center has a 3,000-plus square-foot fitness center with all types of top-notch equipment, men's and women's spas, a lap pool for adults and shallow pool for kids, aerobics facilities, and attended babysiting in the fitness area. Outside, there's a large family park with a one-mile jogging track. In addition to the fitness facilities, the Center has a 50,000-square-foot educational building with a computer lab and special rooms for music and art. High-quality early childhood and after-school care is available. Plus, there's a large auditorium for banquets and lectures, with a serving kitchen. Classes and events for all ages are presented here, too.

To find it: 7300 Hart Lane.
Phone: 512/331-1144.
Accepts: Visa, MC, Amex.
Hours: Mon.-Thurs. 5:30 a.m. to 10 p.m., Fri. 5:30 a.m. to 5 p.m., Sat. 12:30-6 p.m., Sun. 8 a.m. to 7 p.m.

22 El Arroyo.

This local chain of casual Tex-Mex restaurants has been serving up Austin's favorite foods for more than a decade in an atmosphere dubbed "early tacky". Now with three locations and catering service, El Arroyo is never far away when you get a hankering for your favorite tacos, enchiladas and other Mexican specialties.

El Arroyo serves lunch and dinner daily and breakfast on weekends until 3 p.m. For breakfast, try the migas or the tamale omelette, which, according to the menu, sounds great and tastes even better. All breakfast entrees are served with potatoes, napalitos (cactus), and beans.

If you've come in for lunch or dinner, you can't go wrong with the spinach enchiladas or Del Mar enchiladas stuffed with crab and shrimp. Of course, more traditional Mexican entrees are available, from combos like the Federale Special (tamale, enchilada, soft taco, chalupa, rice, beans and a beer) to sizzling fajitas. Or try the barbeque chicken, burgers, or a salad.

El Arroyo Catering brings your favorite menu items to your special event, from an array of appetizers to buffet entrees to dessert. In addition to the food, El Arroyo can provide a margarita, wine and beer bar, and even will arrange for entertainment.

Once you've become an El Arroyo regular, take home a T-shirt or baseball cap to declare your loyalty.

To find it: 1624 W. Fifth, Austin; 301 E. Hwy. 79, Round Rock; 7032 Wood Hollow Drive.
Phone: 512/474-1222 (5th St.), 345-TACO (Far West), 310-1992 (Round Rock).
Accepts: Major credit cards.
Hours: Mon.-Tue., 11 a.m. to 10 p.m.; Wed.-Thu., 11 a.m. to 11 p.m.; Fri., 11 a.m. to midnight; Sat. 10 a.m. to midnight; Sun. 10 a.m. to 10 p.m.
w w w . d i t c h . c o m

19 County Line Restaurants.

Both County Line locations serve excellent barbecue —from ribs to brisket to chicken and more — in a fun atmosphere reminiscent of a Texas roadhouse.

County Line on the Hill. Located in a historic rock building perched on one of the highest hills in the area, this County Line offers a 20-mile view of the Texas Hill country. The sunsets are spectacular, and so is the food, including a full line of grilled items such as steak, fish and kabobs.

To find it: 6500 W. Bee Caves Road.
Phone: 512/327-1742.
Accepts: All major credit cards.
Hours: Dinner only, seven days a week.
Notable: Entire restaurant may be reserved for private luncheons, seven days a week.

County Line on the Lake. Set in an old lake lodge, this County Line is

right on the water. Cocktails on the lower deck are a must, and the lower dining area has five huge windows overlooking the deck and lake. Specialties include smoked prime rib and smoked pork tenderloin.

To find it: 5204 F.M. 2222.
Phone: 512/346-3664.
Accepts: All major credit cards.
Hours: Lunch and dinner, seven days a week.
Notable: Accessible by boat. Private party room seats 20-60.

10 **Mirabelle.** The interplay of food and wine takes center stage at this neighborhood restaurant, which has become quite popular. Mirabelle's dinner menu is specifically designed to be paired with the restaurant's extensive wine list for a terrific dining experience. The contemporary American cuisine is spiced with various world flavors, including French, Italian, Asian and Southwestern. Among the taste-tempting dishes are the picadillo empanedas, the blackened Gulf shrimp with Gorgonzola cream and the Mushroom-crusted lamb with Balsamic jus. Or come for brunch and try the Eggs Benedict with citrus hollandaise or the apple-stuffed French toast. The Mediterranean-style decor showcases the work of local artists. Private rooms can accommodate up to 60 people.

To find it: 8127 Mesa Drive.
Phone: 512/346-7900.
Accepts: Visa, MC, Amex, Diners.
Hours: Lunch served 11 a.m. to 2 p.m. Mon.-Fri. Dinner 5:30-9:30 p.m. Mon.-Thurs., 5:30-10 p.m. Fri.-Sat. Sunday Brunch 10:30 a.m. to 2 p.m.
Notable: *Wine Spectator's* Award of Excellence for one of most outstanding restaurant an wine lists in the world. Local critics praise.

11 **Carl Smith, Registered Massage Therapist.**
Are you always looking for a deep-tissue massage that is strong enough to ease your muscle strain without the therapist digging into your body with his or her elbows?

Fewer than 10 massage therapists in Austin practice Tuina, the art of oriental massage. This type of therapy is excellent for those who work long hours in front of a computer, sit in endless meetings, or have old, recurring injuries. Tuina is also excellent for any type of jaw or teeth grinding problems (TMJ) and migraines.

He reports success in reducing the curve of scoliosis and painful tension. He also has had success in removing the pain of sciatica.

If you are concerned about your physical and mental well-being, or if you have an old neck or back injury that flares up, Carl Smith is your man.

Massage is available in his office, or in your home or office. Chair massage is available for corporate clients or small offices. Mention *Austin's Best* for a special offer.

To find it: 4131 Spicewood Springs, Building K.
Phone: 512/848-5493, 343-9664.
Fax: 512/343-6047.
Accepts: Checks.
Hours: Flexible hours, by appointment only.
Notable: One of few Austin therapists versed in Tuina, the art of oriental massage.

5 **Run Tex**
Gateway Market.
Phone: 512/472-3254 (Town Lake), 343-1164 (Gateway Market).
Hours: Monday to Friday 10 a.m. to 8 p.m.; Saturday 9 a.m. to 6 p.m.; Sunday 1-4 p.m.
Notable: Baby joggers for rent. Highly knowledgeable staff. Full slate of training programs, classes, and events. Refer to page 74 for more details.

14 Richard Allan Silk Floral.

They may look natural, but look again. The flowers, plants and trees here are fashioned of silk, but they are as realistic-looking as a vase of cut flowers or a just-watered ficus tree. That's why so many of Austin's finest interior designers turn to Richard Allan when they need a special silk arrangement or plant.

The floral products here range from natural-stem silk flowers to dried flowers to a range of trees, including ficus, ming aralia, mango and areca palms. And although this shop is best known for its silk plants and flowers, it has expanded its offerings to include decorative accessories, occasional tables, artwork, and antiques.

You'll find mirrors, prints and original art, all beautifully framed. Table, floor and candlestick lamps. And accessories like bookends, boxes, statuary, animals and candles.

If you don't find just what you're looking for, speak to the expert sales staff. Trained in interior design, especially floral and plant accessorization, they can help direct you to the right pieces for your home. Or if you're looking for something completely unique, they can help you design a one-of-a-kind original. Richard Allan custom-makes silk plants, trees and floral arrangements to fit your decor and space requirements. Even if you're already working with an interior designer, Richard Allan's staff can help. Ask for a complimentary, in-home or -office consultation.

To find it: 2945 W. Anderson Lane.
Phone: 512/452-1096.
Accepts: MC, Visa, Amex, Discover. Personal checks with ID.
Hours: Monday-Friday 9 a.m. to 6 p.m. Saturday 10 a.m. to 5 p.m. Open holidays except Christmas and New Year's.
Notable: Highest-quality, natural-looking silk plants and florals. Decorative accessories. Custom-manufactured silk plants, trees and florals.

13 **Grapevine Market.** Wine and food lovers will find paradise here. Grapevine Market boasts a huge selection of wines, including the largest array of Italian wines in America. Even those on a budget will find the right bottle, because Grapevine Market stocks the largest quantities of lower-end wine in the city. For aficionados of Scotch whisky, there's an enormous selection spanning at least 150 differ-

ent makers. Not to mention a huge variety of beers. A walk-in humidor keeps fine cigars at their best. And grab some gourmet take-out from the in-house chef, or fashion your own from the selection of hormone-free, range-fed beef; caviar; paté; chocolate; coffees; vinegars; and oils.

To find it: 7938 Great Northern Blvd.
Phone: 512/323-5900.
Accepts: MC, Visa, Discover, Amex. Personal checks with ID.
Hours: Monday-Saturday 10 a.m. to 9 p.m. Open holidays except Christmas, New Year's and Thanksgiving.
Notable: Extraordinary array of wines. Fourteen-week wine course for customers. Delivery service.

15 **Heirloom Gardens.** A beautiful store that pleases all the senses. Heirloom Gardens is a marriage of the best in heirloom plants and the finest in garden-related products. Owner Kathy Thompson —she's also a degreed horticulturist—likes to call it an

indoor cottage garden, which extends to a charming trellised courtyard of vines and a pond. Wind chimes softly play, herbal and floral scents perfume the air and unique gifts abound. For serious gardeners, there are serious tools from Fiskars and Tools of Maine, as well as potting soils and organic pesticides. Garden journals, books and calendars help keep the green thumbs organized. The garden theme extends to botanical prints, herbal candles and wonderful soaps and lotions. And of course, there are plants, from heirloom roses and herbs to English ivy topiaries and antique bulbs.

To find it: Village Shopping Center, 2700 W. Anderson Lane, Suite 904, Austin.
Phone: 512/451-0241.
Website: www.heirloomgardens. citysearch.com.
Accepts: MC, Visa, Discover. Checks.
Hours: Monday-Saturday 10 a.m. to 5:30 p.m.
Notable: Monthly newsletter. Free potting service. Bridal registry. Friendly service. Gift wrap and shipping.

16 Lonny's Retail and Salon.

Anyone can find the beauty products they're looking for at Lonny's, whether teens on a quest for the latest trendy nail polish to more mature women who want the hairspray their mothers used to use. At the same time, they can have their hair cut, highlighted, colored, permed, or even have an old-fashioned shampoo set, not to mention a relaxing pedicure.

Started 28 years ago by Lonny Morton, this salon later became the city's first retail beauty supply as well. Now, the operation encompasses 3,600 square feet of beauty services and products. The husband-and-wife team of Greg and Jesse Boatright own and operate the business, but visitors also will often see their six-year-old son unpacking boxes and their 10-year-old daughter ringing up sales.

Decorated in corrugated tin and 100-year-old barn wood from Pflugerville, the salon has a clean, yet rustic, feel. The retail area continues the theme with natural stone and navy carpeting. This homey atmosphere is enhanced by the Boatright's hospitality. In the salon, there's always coffee and cake, as well as a galvanized bucket of iced-down sodas.

With such refreshments at hand, and the friendly stylists and other salon personnel to assist you, it's difficult not to have a good time at Lonny's. The old-fashioned values of Lonny and the Boatrights are carried out by the employees, who range in age from 26 to 76. "Our service keeps our clients feeling very special," explains Jesse Boatright.

Besides the attentive, personal service, Lonny's also prides itself on its wide selection of beauty products

and other goodies. Hair products, nail products, skin care and cosmetics line the shelves, along with skin and hair appliances and accessories. Such lines as Sebastian, Alterna, Murad, Matrix, Redken and OPI are well-represented. The shop carries some 80 brands in all, including the

new lines and some that date back to the 1930s.

Gift-shopping is easy at Lonny's, too, what with the selection of body-and-bath goodies, Seasons candles and room sprays — even New Canaan Farms jellies and hot sauces.

One last word on Lonny's — the prices are fantastic. They are the lowest in town, or anywhere! That's why so many out-of-town customers call Lonny's to have their favorite products shipped right to their homes.

To find it: 7797 Burnet Road, Austin, Texas 78757, across from Northcross Mall in the Northstar Home Center.
Phone: 512/454-2619.
Accepts: MC, Visa, Discover. Personal checks with proper ID.
Hours: Weekdays 8 a.m. to 7 p.m. Saturday 8 a.m. to 6 p.m. Sunday 12-5 p.m.
Notable: Both popular and hard-to-find products. Lowest prices. Will ship products anywhere.

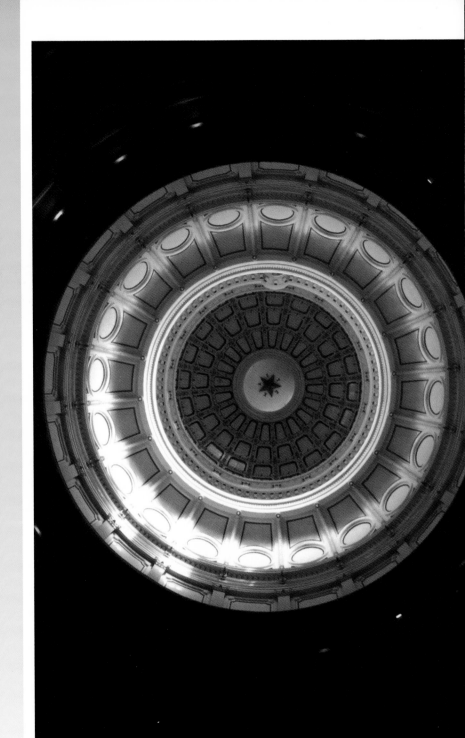

Capital Seal

© James Innes

The Lyndon Baines Johnson Library and Museum

No trip to Austin can be complete without a stop at the LBJ Library and Museum. Located at 2313 Red River Street, the Library is a must-see exhibit of the life and times of the nation's larger-than-life 36th president.

Once inside you'll see many of the most noteworthy pieces of the Johnson Administration in dozens of unique historical displays. The Library can draw from a collection totaling 40 million documents. Two of the most prized permanent exhibits include a collection of gifts from America's allies and a large-scale replica of the Oval Office from the time Johnson occupied the White House -- including the numerous television sets that constantly screened the day's news shows.

History buffs will enjoy the documentaries on Johnson's time in office, including clips that will bring back vivid memories of a turbulent era marked by Vietnam, the war protests, the landmark Civil Rights Movement and Johnson's vision of the Great Society. Two short videos show the man at work, giving you insights into his monumental energy as well as his ever-present sense of humor. A special, 20-minute presentation traces the life of the boy who grew up poor in the Hill Country of Texas and went on to become a U.S. Senator before occupying the White House.

There's also a delightful collection of political cartoons from the '60s— including more than a few that openly poked fun at Johnson himself.

The Museum hosts several special exhibits each year, an added bonus for the repeat visitor. Museum and gift shop are open from 9 AM to 5 PM every day except Christmas. Parking is free and the Museum still bows to Johnson's wishes that all visitors can enter free of charge as well.

61

Moving data at the speed of light. That's what Crossroads Systems Inc. does, and in a world hooked on computer speed, that's something..

You see, many companies and governments have to store huge amounts of data every day. Much of that information is stored on computer tape.

If you've ever copied a file from a computer tape to your hard drive, you can guess how long searching for data on computer tape might take. Forever—or at least it would seem like forever.

Crossroads has changed all that.

The Austin company makes a router—basically, a small electronic box —that converts digital data into light. True to its name, the box routes data from a "storage-area network" —such as tape libraries— and allows people to access that data at fast speeds.

This router is the must-have piece of equipment for those who store mountains of data. And it spawned a hot technology stock, as Crossroads went public in October 1999 to raves from the market. Crossroads offered 3.75 million shares at $18 a share— and the stock had more than quadrupled the offering price by the end of one day's trading, to more than $78.

That excitement is based on Crossroad's fast growth and market share. According to published reports, Crossroads saw its revenues grow almost twelvefold from 1997 to 1999: $1 million to $11.79 million, respectively. Crossroads has an estimated 98 percent of the $13 million router market, which is expected to grow exponentially in coming years.

Company executives have said they believe the market will mushroom to $500 million by 2002.

That's quite a pie to grow into, but Crossroads officials are accustomed to fast growth. Brian Smith and Dale Quisenberry founded the company in the mid-1990s and showed their first product at Comdex, the computer industry's big trade show, in 1996. They started shipping in fall 1997, and by 1998 saw their shipments and revenue grow by 400 percent. At the same time, their payroll jumped from 35 to 60—and has kept on the upswing from there.

Along the way, they have been helped by financing from Silicon Valley Bank and from Austin's own Austin Ventures, which provided most of the company's $18 million in private financing.

It has helped that CEO Brian Smith has a strong faith to help him ride out the tough times—including the time back in 1996 when he realized the company had only $9 in its checking account.

"He doesn't go home and worry about it at night," Bob LiVolsi, senior vice president of sales and marketing, told the *Austin American-Statesman*. "He believes that if you just keep going at it, the Lord's going to take care of it."

The company still faces its share of challenges. Its router fills a niche in the market now, but technology changes quickly. Smith says he's anticipated that. "We're not just here for two years. We've got a forward-looking technology that makes us relevant well into the future."

2 Arbor Car Wash.

Remember the days when cars were washed by hand, not by whirling brushes? You can return to that kind of service at this full-service car wash and lube shop. Each vehicle is washed by hand as it moves through a tunnel, and it emerges sparkling clean. Arbor Car Wash can also give the inside of your car the treatment with its complete detail service. And what about the engine? Need an oil change? The on-site Pennzoil Lube Shop can handle it. And you can fill up your tank with Texaco gasoline. While you wait, kick back and watch the television, which is equipped with satellite programming, or browse the auto accessories on the shelves. You can even buy a birthday card for Grandma.

Address: 10401 Jollyville Road, Austin, Texas 78759.
Phone: 512-346-8050.
Accepts: All major credit cards, Texaco credit card. Personal check with ID.
Hours: Monday to Saturday 8 a.m. to 6 p.m; Sunday 9 a.m. to 5 p.m.

1 The Lamp Shoppe.

Step into The Lamp Shoppe and you'll see a series of vignettes designed to help customers choose lamps and other decorative accessories for their homes. Each tableau skillfully blends lamps, fabrics, artwork, and accessories to demonstrate how customers can add personality to their home by choosing the right mix of things.

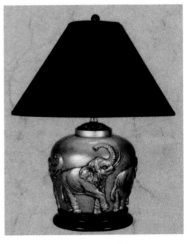

This attention to helping customers make choices doesn't stop with these beautiful examples. Bring in your lamp for a proper shade fitting, from the best and largest selection of shades in Austin. Or have the shop craft a custom lamp from musical instruments, cowboy boots, deer antlers, or anything your imagination desires.

To find it: 10710 Research Blvd., Austin, Texas 78759.
Phone: 512/345-1609.
Fax: 512/345-8980.
Accepts: MC, Visa, Discover, Amex. Personal checks.
Hours: Monday-Saturday 10 a.m. to 6 p.m. Open holidays except July Fourth, Thanksgiving and Christmas.
Notable: Personal attention when choosing lamps or fitting new shades. Custom lamps and lamp repair.

63

Magic of the City (detail)
By Linda Dumont

17 **Husbands for Hire.** This is the company to call when you need home repairs, handyman services or remodeling. Every home needs occasional repairs, and every homeowner needs to know that there is a company they can trust to take care of the job properly.

If you don't have the time or the skills to tackle home repairs yourself, give Husbands for Hire a call. The company has been in business for more than 10 years providing qualified, screened service contractors who are fully insured and offer a one-year warranty on all labor performed. Whether it's a faucet replacement or a full room remodel, when you call Husbands for Hire, your project will be taken care of by a home repair professional. Mention this listing and receive a 10 percent discount on your labor (up to $250).

Address: 8711 Burnet Road, Suite A-11, Austin, Texas, 78757.
Phone: 512/451-1817.
Fax: 512/451-2594.
Accepts: MC, Visa, Amex, Discover. Personal checks.
By appointment only.

21 **The Kosher Store.** With growing numbers of Jewish families in Austin, there also has been a growing need for an all-kosher restaurant and store. Tracy Cross developed this store-within-a-store (it's housed in the Far West H-E-B) with the full support of the Rabbinical Council of Austin. Cross says The Kosher Store has been so well-received, it now is a selling point for families wanting to relocate to Austin. "With all the high-tech companies that have located or are stationed in the Austin area, we have become a valuable service," he says. "People who work in the industry from California, New York, Chicago, and Florida—many of them are Jewish, and they keep kosher. Now they have a restaurant away from home."

The Kosher Store also has made it easier for families to keep kosher in Austin. Before, there were no places to buy fresh kosher meat. The Kosher Store not only has kosher meat, but a kosher coffee bar, kosher bakery, and a kosher deli. The entire package is set inside an H-E-B store, making H-E-B the first grocery chain in Texas to have a complete kosher store within a store.

To find it: 7015 Village Center Drive in the Far West H-E-B.
Phone: 512/502-8459.
Accepts: All major credit cards. Personal checks.
Hours: Sunday to Thursday 8 a.m. to 8 p.m. Friday 8 a.m. to 5 p.m. Closed Saturday. Normal holiday hours; call ahead to inquire.
Notable: Only complete kosher store in Austin.

3 **Clarksville Pottery.** Founded more than 20 years ago as a small pottery studio in the historic Austin neighborhood of Clarksville, Clarksville Pottery & Galleries has grown to become one of the top American craft galleries in the nation. (See complete listing in the Central section).

To find it: 9722 Great Hills Trail, in Arboretum Market near Saks.
Phone: 512/794-8580.
Accepts: Visa, MC, Amex, Discover. Personal checks with proper ID.
Hours: Monday to Saturday 10 a.m. to 6:30 p.m., except open until 8 p.m. Thursday; Sunday 12-6 p.m.
Notable: Nationally known gallery of fine American craft. Hand-painted gift wrap.

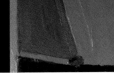

4 Founded by John Mackey, Craig Weller and Mark Skiles, Whole Foods Market proved its mettle early on. Memorial Day 1981, the chain's first store flooded. The entire inventory and most of its equipment were destroyed. But Whole Foods rebuilt, with the help of many loyal customers, and in time became a phenomenon. Now the nation's leading retailer of organic, natural, and environmentally friendly foods, Whole Foods has won kudos for its products, but also for its team management style; *Fortune* magazine has named it one of the best 100 companies to work for.

Now Whole Foods not only has a chain of stores, but also three house brands, each with a range of products specially selected for their natural origins and high quality. Many of the premium-label products are made by small, regional companies that care about quality.

Along the way, Whole Foods has remained committed to its mission of providing organically grown and other natural foods. By expanding the market for these products, the company has helped to boost production of them, and, in turn, aided organic farmers and growers. The company also has shown its commitment to its communities by donating 5 percent of after-tax profits to non-profit organizations, and by paying employees up to 20 hours each year for volunteer work.

It's all part of the Whole Foods philosophy of supporting the health, well-being, and healing of people and the planet. With its commitment to natural products and to empowering its people, Whole Foods is leading the way to a cleaner, healthier, happier world.

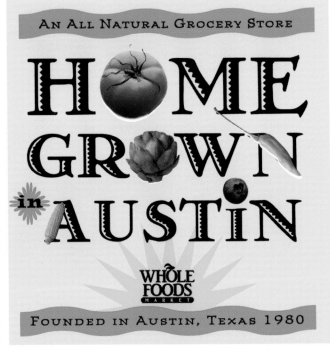

AN ALL NATURAL GROCERY STORE

HOME GROWN in AUSTIN

WHOLE FOODS MARKET

FOUNDED IN AUSTIN, TEXAS 1980

Asian gifts imported from China, Japan and Vietnam add their own spice to the selection.

The shopping and dining is made even more enjoyable by a beautiful garden patio, one of the best in the city, and by the live music every Friday and Saturday nights. So when you're craving a healthy Vietnamese meal—or a latté or a breakfast taco or a fantastic sandwich—or need to shop for someone special, come to Triumph. You'll be satisfied.

12 **Triumph Cafe & Gift Shop.** Soon after Truc Nguyen started this coffee-and-pastry shop, his customers persuaded him to add Vietnamese food to the menu. And this unique, eclectic combination—Vietnamese restaurant, coffee house and gift shop—was born.

Now, it's possible to visit Triumph for a breakfast bagel or croissant, a luncheon sandwich served on homemade European flatbread, and a Vietnamese dinner of spring rolls, vermicelli, noodle soup, stir fried noodle, and steamed rice dishes. And a specialty espresso drink, hot tea or chai along with dessert.

Between meals, you can drop by to shop for house-roasted coffee beans and other gifts. Try the house blend, "Glorious Morning," which is well-known in town, or one of the many other blends Triumph sells to various upscale restaurants and hotels in the area. Other unique gifts on hand include individually hand-painted silk ties, available at art galleries and museum shops elsewhere, but sold in Austin only at Triumph.

To find it: 3808 Spicewood Springs Road.

Phone: 512/343-1875.
Accepts: All major credit cards. Personal checks.
Hours: 7 a.m. to 9 p.m. Monday-Thursday; 7 a.m. to 11 p.m. Friday; 8 a.m. to 11 p.m. Saturday; 9 a.m. to 3 p.m. Sunday.
Notable: Live music Fridays and Saturdays. Gift shop with exclusive hand-painted silk ties, unique Asian gifts, house-roasted coffee beans. One of the best patios in town.

Hubcap Annie's tale has been told so many times, it's a permanent part of Austin folklore. But that doesn't mean it's not worth telling again.

Our story begins in 1980, when Barbara Sanders (better known as Annie) was convinced to follow in her hubcap-collecting sister's footsteps and open a shop catering to the pothole victim.

Throwing caution to the wind, she left the security of the legal profession to begin an education in hubcaps. Her first challenge was to convince a landlord that she could pay the rent selling hubcaps. With lots of support from family and friends, she found success.

Over the years, she has amassed an ever growing and changing collection of hubcaps, tires and wheels. Closely guarding her integrity, she takes the driver's license numbers from all sellers and works closely with the Auto theft division of the Austin Police Department.

Today, because of her notoriety, she receives faraway requests for special, hard to find hubcaps-and 99 percent of the time can fill them. Her favorite question? When someone says, "I know you don't have it but...then she says, "How many do you need?"

Now, she and her business have fused into one. Even all six of her grandchildren call her hubcap Annie. Not only is she an Austin celebrity, she is a landmark too.

9 Hubcap Annie. If you hit a pothole and dent a wheel, lose or break a hubcap, any Austinite can tell you where to go. Hubcap Annie.

At this Lamar Boulevard shop, you will find any hubcap you happen to need. Owner Barbara Sanders knows more about wheels and hubcaps than anyone in town does, and she is intimately familiar with her inventory. She can describe practically any hubcap at will.

She has her own dream team comprised of employees who are well trained and experienced in meeting customer needs. Or you can get into hubcap trading yourself. Just bring in any hubcap you may have and Annie will usually buy it or give you a trade-in towards your purchase.

To top it off, they cheerfully and expertly install your hubcaps on site and for free. Now that's a real service.

To find it: 10104 N. Lamar Blvd.
Phone: 512-837-0067.
Hours: Mon-Fri 9:00 am-5: 30pm Sat. 9:00am-3:00pm Closed Sunday.
Accepts: Cash, checks, Visa MasterCard and Discover.

Notable: Huge inventory of new and used hubcaps and factory stock wheels. Free installation of hubcaps with purchase. Plus, friendly service and a great atmosphere-how's that for a hubcap shop?

69

South Austin

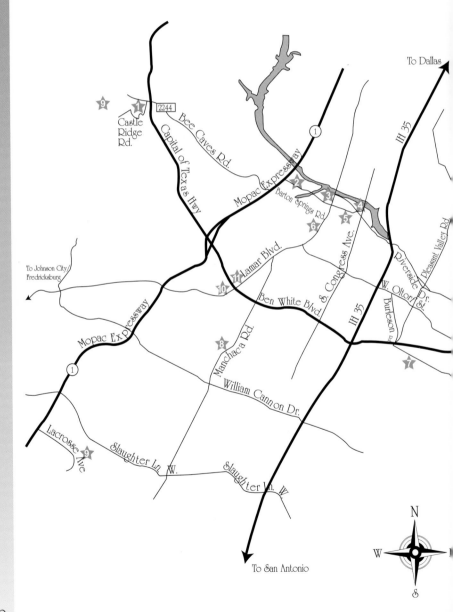

To Dallas

2244

Castle
Ridge
Rd.

Bee Caves Rd.

Capital of Texas Hwy

Mopac Expressway

Barton Springs Rd.

IH 35

Lamar Blvd.

S. Congress Ave.

Riverside Dr.

Pleasant Valley Rd.

To Johnson City/
Fredricksburg

Ben White Blvd.

W. Oltorf St.

Burleson Rd.

Mopac Expressway

Manchaca Rd.

IH 35

William Cannon Dr.

Lacrosse Ave

Slaughter Ln. W.

Slaughter Ln. W.

To San Antonio

N
W   E
S

A surge of redevelopment has given South Austin a hip edge, especially along South Congress Avenue where you can browse funky shops and sample some great Tex-Mex. Stop by Town Lake and pay homage to the statue of Austin's king of music, Stevie Ray Vaughan, and then go for a walk along the shore, a mecca for the city's runners, walkers and bikers. Zilker Park, one of the city's best, is a few blocks away. Or visit the Austin Zoo or Austin Nature Center— kids love them.

Hamilton Pool

Hundreds of years ago, the enormous grotto of an underground, Hill Country lake collapsed, creating one of the most delightful swimming holes in America. Located 20 miles west of Austin near Highway 71, this is a great place for weary travellers to stop and spend some quality time - or as a fun destination for the whole family.

There are few places to swim that offer such a scenic setting as Hamilton Pool. This swimming area has a stunning, 65-foot waterfall, sandy shores and an awe-inspiring set of rock formations that circle the water's edge and date back to the great collapse. Fed by underground streams, the water is clear and fresh.

Located at 24300 Hamilton Pool Road in the town of Bee Cave, the only drawback about Hamilton Pool is its limited size. If you're planning to swim, make sure you're among the first 100 cars to show up. In order to protect the pool's sensitive ecosystem, park officials close the entrance once they hit their maximum occupancy, so the earlier you get there the better your chances of getting inside.

So call ahead — 512-264-2740 — if you feel that you may be running late. The pool is also closed in the event of heavy rains. Now a Travis County Park, visitors are charged $5 per car. Hamilton Pool is open daily.

Paul Carrozza is the *Runner's World* shoe editor, and his staff is equally qualified to help select the best shoes and apparel for each customer.

Training programs available through RunTex include free classes, including track workouts offered five days a week at various locations for all levels of runners. For nominal fees, RunTex offers beginner classes and race training programs. And if you're sponsoring a race or meet, RunTex offers management and promotion that can boost the proceeds for your charity. For more information on programs and services, visit RunTex's informative website listed below.

To find it: 422 W. Riverside Drive, near Town Lake. Or No. 140 in Gateway Market.
Phone: 512/472-3254 (Town Lake), 343-1164 (Gateway Market).
Online: www.runtex.com
Accepts: Major credit cards. Personal checks with proper ID.
Hours: Monday to Friday 10 a.m. to 8 p.m.; Saturday 9 a.m. to 6 p.m. Sunday 1-4 p.m.
Notable: Baby joggers for rent. Highly knowledgeable staff. Full slate of training programs, classes, and events.

4 **RunTex.** If you knew that this home-grown chain has been described by *Runner's World* as the best running store in the world, then you'd probably have high expectations on your first visit.

Well, at RunTex, you won't be disappointed. Because this store is no longer simply a retail outlet. It's a multi-service organization that provides training programs, clinics, seminars, information services, race organization, and a meeting place for runners and walkers.

Of course you'll find hundreds of styles and sizes of running shoes, along with a huge assortment of running apparel, accessories and nutritional supplements. There's even merchandise specifically created for children. To help make your selection, owners Paul and Sheila Carrozza and their staff of 25-plus employees are there to help. And they know what they're talking about—all are runners or triathletes themselves.

3 **El Sol y La Luna.** This cozy, casual, art-lined café if your ticket to award-winning Mexican specialties. El Sol y La Luna has captured rave reviews and is consistently chosen as one of Austin's favorite restaurants. It's also among *Hispanic Magazine*'s 50 Best Hispanic Restaurants nationwide.

Come during the warm months and relax on the patio with a fresh-squeezed lemonade or a refreshing sangria. When it's cold outside, warm up with a cup of Mexican hot chocolate.

And beverages are just the beginning. Breakfast is served all day, whether migas or huevos motuleños or the best pozole in town. Or stop by for a coffee break and a breakfast taco, standouts in a city full of them.

If you're hankering for a crispy taco or enchilada, you've come to the right place as well. The enchiladas rojas are award-winners. Or try one of El Sol y La Luna's many specialties, including some of the finest interior Mexican food around. The chicken molé is fabulous, and there are vegetarian choices, too.

On Fridays and Saturdays, live Latin American music adds a festive touch to an evening. But even if you're visiting during the day or on a weeknight, the great food and service and the casual atmosphere make any meal a celebration.

To find it: 1224 S. Congress Ave.
Phone: 512/444-7770.
Accepts: All major credit cards.
Hours: Sun.-Tues.   7 a.m. to 3 p.m.;
Wed.-Sat.   7 a.m. to 10 p.m.
Notable: Try the pozole, the molé, the enchiladas rojas, and every item on the breakfast menu. Live Latin American music on Friday and Saturday evenings.

Hike and Bike Trails

The generally friendly climate and lovely setting combine to make Austin a city for the outdoors. And the City of Austin has done its part to provide facilities for those who like to bike, hike, or simply stroll a pretty path.

One of the most visible—and popular—of the trails is the 10-mile Town Lake Walk and Bikeway. Strung along Town Lake through the center of the city, this trail attracts thousands every day with its beautiful view of the lake and the skyline on both sides. In the spring, the sight is especially beautiful. More than 3,000 trees and shrubs line the trail, including redbuds, cherry trees, plum trees, peach trees, and a host of endangered Texas species. When the trees are in bloom, they lend a special sweetness to the landscape; you almost feel as if you're walking through a picture postcard.

The trail starts at the Congress Avenue bridge on the south side of the lake. It runs west into Zilker Park and then crosses the lake under MoPac, and continues east past Fiesta Gardens to Longhorn Dam, where it crosses back over. Walkers, runners, and cyclists are welcome. If you'd like to venture out with a group, call the Sierra Club 512/445-6223 about its weekly hike around Town Lake.

Mountain bikers and hikers like the Barton Creek Greenbelt, which runs along the creek upward for eight miles from the Barton Springs pool in Zilker Park. The terrain is rugged, and depending upon recent rainfall, you may have to wade through water because the trail crosses the creek several times. At some points on this trail, there's even enough topography for climbers. The scenery is Hill Country limestone and rapids, when the creek is running. Spring-fed swimming holes also provide visual interest. In spring, wildflowers bloom, and bird-watching isn't bad in any season.

Other trails in the city include the Shoal Creek Hike and Bike Trail, which runs three miles from Town Lake up to West 38th Street along Shoal Creek and Lamar Boulevard. The Waller Creek Walkway also attracts its share of joggers; it runs from Town Lake to the University of Texas. Three shorter trails—the Johnson Creek and Boggy Creek hike and bike trails and the Blunn Creek Preserve—each are around a mile long. The Forest Ridge Nature Preserve west of Loop 360 just south of Spicewood Springs Road offers a hiking trail through a golden-cheeked warbler habitat; you will find the trail on the east end of the parking lot closest to the road.

Mountain bikers often use the Rocky Creek Mountain Bike Ranch on F.M. 153 near Smithville. The 1,200-acre ranch has more than 30 miles of trails. The varying terrain provides a variety of experiences, and the trails are graded by difficulty. The expert trails truly are challenging; ex-world champion Lance Armstrong trains here. A cafe provides post-riding refreshments and live music on weekends. There's a daily fee; call 512/237-3112 for information.

In South Austin, there's a Veloway, a winding path just for bicyclists and skaters. It lies just adjacent to the Lady Bird Johnson Wildflower Center. The Veloway is open daily, and there's no admission.

© James Innes

Children's Advocacy Center.

In 1990, a 22-month-old boy, Christopher Wohlers, died a horrible death from abuse. Outraged Austin citizens demanded a better system for protecting young victims. And the Child Protection Team and Children's Advocacy Center Inc. were born.

At the time, several agencies were very committed to protecting children and were remarkably coopera-

Sandra Martin/Executive Director Travis County Children's Advocacy Center Austin

Center, children with suspected abuse are nurtured in a home-like environment. The Child Protection Team, composed of representatives of the various investigating agencies in child abuse, investigate the abuse as a unit, eliminating the need for telling and retelling of traumatic events. Medical exams, treatment and follow-up care are provided by specialists. The center makes sure that children and their families receive counseling, and follows up and tracks cases through the courts. Children and parents even have an opportunity to receive a court orientation. This can relieve s their anxieties about doing so.

Those interested in helping the Children's Advocacy Center can participate by donating money, volunteering their time, serving as a child advocate or donating needed equipment or supplies. To get involved, call or write using the information below.

tive with one another. But despite their best intentions, these agencies often ended up re-victimizing the children, who were often forced to retell their story many times to the various different agencies investigating the abuse. The children received little or no counseling to help them recover from their trauma, and were at great risk of further violence and victimization.

Now, at the Children's Advocacy

To find it: 1110 E. 32nd Street, Austin, Texas 78722.
Phone: 512/472-1164; 24-hour child abuse hotline, 800/252-5400.
Fax: 512/472-1167.
Email: smartin@traviscountycac.org.
Notable: Serves children who are victims of sexual abuse, serious physical injury, and/or witness to a violent crime—in a child-friendly, specially equipped and designed home.

© James Innes

5 The Filling Station.

Famous for their huge, three-quarter-pound hamburgers since 1975, this restaurant also offers an eclectic menu of crisp salads, tender chicken-fried steak, and sizzling fajitas. All of the food is prepared in-house, daily. Get started with an tune-up from the full bar, and finish off your meal with one of the deli-

cious dessert selections. Entrees start at $4.25. Whatever you order, you'll feel comfortable in this casual, fun atmosphere of old car and gas-station memorabilia. Reservations are accepted, but unnecessary. The Filling Station is happy to open its banquet room for private get-togethers of up to 45 people.

To find it: 801 Barton Sporings Road.
Phone: 512/477-1022.
Email: fsaustin@aol.com.
Accepts: Visa, MC, Discover, Amex, Diners.
Hours: Monday-Thursday 11 a.m. to midnight; Friday-Saturday, 11 a.m. to 2 a.m.; Sunday noon to midnight.
Notable: Authentic car and gas-station memorabilia, including a 1924 Model T Ford "Banana Wagon". Fresh ingredients used in all menu offerings. Child's menu available.

1 Raymond Oukrop, D.D.S.

Dr. Oukrop offers the full spectrum of general dentistry, but his specialties are cosmetic and aesthetic services. He can provide a beautiful smile through bonding, veneer and other modalities. He also can perform full-mouth rehabilitation for individuals with overbites, severe loss of teeth strength, or retruded lower jaws that cause a loss of facial vertical dimension. Individuals with these problems often find they lead to a compromised physical, physiological and aesthetic position. The initial consultation is free. Call for an appointment at his comfortably furnished South Austin office.

Address: 609 Castle Ridge Road, Suite 326, Austin, Texas 78746. On the southwest corner at Bee Caves/620.
Phone: 512/327-5977, 327-5979.
Accepts: MC, Visa, Discover. Personal checks.
Hours: Monday to Thursday 8:30 a.m. to noon and 2-4 p.m; Friday 8:30 a.m. to noon.

6 Metropolitan Gallery.

Behind the door of a renovated frame house on Lamar is this oasis of art that caters to each client's personal tastes and pocketbook. Owner Jennie Branch will visit your home or office and then find the appropriate pieces to complement your decor and personality. Her expert eye comes at no charge, and she frequently can find art at better prices than you could on your own.

Or just come by to browse. Metropolitan Gallery's artists—including *Austin's Best* artist Linda Dumont— work in every style and medium. Here you can find art from contemporary to traditional, oil paintings to photography, bronze sculpture to blown glass. And whether you want an historically significant work of art or just a popular print, Branch can find it for you through art brokers, auction houses, or publishers worldwide.

To find it: 903 South Lamar.
Phone: 512/326-1611.
Accepts: MC, Visa, Amex. Personal checks.
Hours: Monday-Friday, 10 a.m. to 6 p.m. Saturday 12-5 p.m. Or by appointment at home or in office.
Notable: No charge for consulting. Can find or even commission art. Special services include custom framing, appraisals, crating and shipping, lighting and professional installation.

81

10 **Central Market.** Here's a store for people who love to eat, and if they like to cook, too— well, so much the better. It's a gourmand's delight, from the 500 varieties of produce to 2,000 labels of wine. The fresh fish and seafood department boasts the best selection west of the Mississippi, and the meat and poultry cases show off the best variety in town. The European-style bakery is a yeasty-smelling heaven of more than 60 different bread varieties, and an in-house tortilleria produces a a variety of special creations. Or how about the Pastry shop, with its incomparable variety of sweet treats? In the deli, you can find genuine Italian prosciutto, smoked salmon, pate, and more. If you're a cheese lover, there's no better place to find that special variety. And the specialty foods aisles are stocked with more than 13,000 products from around the world, to complete the most basic or most exotic dish.

Don't feel like cooking? Stop by Cafe on the Run, where you'll find chef-prepared salads and sandwiches, as well as main-and side-dish fare to take home. Or relax at the Central Market Cafe, which showcases the best of the store's fresh ingredients. Besides a complete menu, the cafe offers daily specials and quick-to-pick-up sandwiches.

To find it: 4477 S. Lamar Blvd. at Ben White. (Central location, page 40)
Phone: 512/899-4300 south.
Accepts: MC, Visa, Discover, Amex, debit cards. Personal checks.
Hours: Store: 9 a.m. to 9 p.m. daily.
Cafe: Sunday-Thursday 7 a.m. to 10 p.m.; Friday-Saturday 7 a.m. to 11 p.m.
Notable: Gargantuan selection of all foodstuffs, from produce and meats to seafood and wine. Specialty products from around the world. In-house baked goods. Cooking school.

2 **Green Mesquite BBQ & More.** The barbeque and the atmosphere here has a 50-year-old-plus pedigree. It started out as a place called "Dunks" that served burgers and watermelon, and you could sit on the patio under the pecan trees and count fireflies. Jerry Jacobs and his wife Bobbie took over after World War II, and Jerry endured long days and nights to smoke his brisket 16 hours (at least). His knack for remembering names kept a lot of people coming back, and even during the dark days of segregation, anyone could get served here as long as they followed the house requirement to be polite.

The Jacobs turned over their restaurant some 30-odd years later to Harold Tiedt, who in turn sold it to a fellow called Pee Wee, who gave the place his name. He started the tradition of live music on the patio, inviting many of those we now watch on Austin City Limits to play.

Since 1988, Tom and Liz Davis have been carrying the torch here. The brisket still smokes 16 hours or more. The same patio still serves as a stage for great live music on weekends, including traditional bluegrass on Sundays. Pecan trees still arch overhead and you can still count fireflies at no extra charge. The Davises still try to remember everyone's name, and everyone is still welcome as long as they are polite. Remember to say hello when you come and goodbye when you have to leave, and enjoy your barbeque or burger while you're here.

To find it: 1400 Barton Springs Road.
Phone: 512/479-0485
Accepts: MC/Amex/Visa/Diners, Discover, Local checks.
Hours: 11a.m.-10p.m. 7 days a week
Notable: Long-smoked brisket. Live music on the patio. Annual fiddle contest each fall.

© James Innes

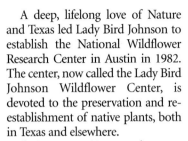

A deep, lifelong love of Nature and Texas led Lady Bird Johnson to establish the National Wildflower Research Center in Austin in 1982. The center, now called the Lady Bird Johnson Wildflower Center, is devoted to the preservation and re-establishment of native plants, both in Texas and elsewhere.

"I just want Texas to keep on looking like Texas," Mrs. Johnson told *Texas Monthly* in 1994.

To an uneducated observer, the former First Lady's untiring work on behalf of the Center and its cause may seem quixotic. After all, wild-flowers are just wildflowers.

But to one more familiar with Mrs. Johnson's life and works, her campaign for native plants and wild-flowers seems only natural. She has had a special bond with nature since her mother died when she was only five years old. Ever since her maiden Aunt Effie, who came to help raise the young Lady Bird, taught her charge how to listen to the wind in the pine trees and look for the beauty in a meadow, Mrs. Johnson has loved nature and done all she could to help others appreciate its beauty.

In Washington, the First Lady put together a committee of women to beautify the capital. Visitors to the city today can see this group's legacy: thousands of tulips, daffodils and other bulbs, as well as cherry trees and dogwoods, planted along the Potomac, near the monuments and even in blighted neighborhoods.

Once back in Texas, she turned her full energies to bringing beauty to her native state, which had changed while she was away. Fields, flowers and trees had been taken over by cookie-cutter housing devel-

opments and chain restaurants. She spent about five years helping Austin develop the hike-and-bike trail along Town Lake, now used daily by thousands of citizens. And, of course, she gave the city her gift of

the Wildflower Center.

Mrs. Johnson gave 60 acres and $125,000 in seed capital to launch the Center, which now serves as a clearinghouse of information for people all over the country. In 1995, the Center moved into a new, larger facility, and in 1997, it was renamed the Lady Bird Johnson Wildflower Center for her 85th birthday.

So her legacy grows, as states across the country turn to planting wildflowers along their highways and Texans, Mississippians and Kansans alike plant native species in their yards. "If we can get people to see the beauty of the native flora of their own corner of the world with caring eyes, then I'll be real happy," Mrs. Johnson said in 1994.

Well, then, Mrs. Johnson, real happy is what you ought to be.

Wild Ideas: The Store to look for garden-inspired gifts for yourself or a special gardener in your life. And no visit would be complete without a snack at the Wildflower Cafe, which offers soups, salads, sandwiches—and a few of Mrs. Johnson's favorite recipes.

To find it: 4801 La Crosse Ave.

Phone: 512/292-4200

9   Lady Bird Johnson Wildflower Center.

It's an arboretum. A demonstration garden. A garden-themed gift shop. A casual cafe. But most of all, this is a celebration of native plants—their environmental necessity, economic value and, of course, natural beauty.

Founded in 1982 by Lady Bird Johnson and the late actress Helen Hayes, the Wildflower Center has grown in size, scope and reputation since then. It has remained true to its goal of showcasing native plants and educating the public about them.

On a stroll through the grounds, visitors can simply enjoy the lovely botanical gardens, fountains and buildings. Those who want to dig deeper will discover that the entire Center pays homage to Central Texas, incorporating native building materials and traditional architecture, as well as indigenous plants.

The Center hopes you will be inspired to take home some of the ideas highlighted in the demonstration gardens. And that you'll visit

Accepts: MC, Visa, Amex, Discover.
Hours: Grounds open Tuesdays-Sundays 9 a.m. to 5:30 p.m.
Visitors Gallery open Tuesdays-Sundays 9 a.m. to 4 p.m.; Sundays 1-4 p.m.
Wild Ideas: The Store open Thursdays-Saturdays 9 a.m. to 5:30 p.m.; Sundays 1-4 p.m. **Wildflower Cafe** open Tuesdays-Saturdays 10 a.m. to 4 p.m.; Sundays 11 a.m. to 4 p.m. **Little House** open Saturdays 10 a.m. to noon and 1-4 p.m.; Sundays 1-4 p.m.
Notable: Native plants and native places. Kid-friendly.

© James Innes

ATTRACTIONS:
Barton Springs

Barton Springs Pool is more than a swimming hole filled with perpetually refreshing spring water. It is a feature of regional folklore from pre-colonial times to the modern era. The history of Barton Springs is, in a sense, a microcosm of the city's heritage.

Native Americans camped at Barton Springs, and Spanish explorers rested on its banks. A Texas pioneer, William "Uncle Billy" Barton set up his homestead on the banks of the spring. Later, its waters, pumped up naturally from underground at the rate of 35 million gallons per day at a perpetual 68 degrees, powered sawmills and flour mills.

Just after the Civil War, Barton Springs' identity as a swimming hole began to form. It became a popular swimming spot for men and boys, and by 1880, the women got into the act with a swimming club of their own. By the early 20th century, swimming here was so popular that University of Texas students could substitute it for gym class.

Along the way, the land changed hands from its original homesteader several times, ending up as part of the holdings of Col. A.J. Zilker, who gave the property to the city in 1917. It remains part of Zilker Park, the city's largest, today.

Barton Springs enjoyed its status as a peaceful swimming hole for many years. But in modern times it has symbolized the local debate between environmentalists and developers. Environmentalists have fought bitterly against development that would affect the springs and its special species, a rare salamander found only here. Developers, of course, have fought back. Through it all, Barton Springs has been closed and reopened repeatedly. Today, thankfully, it is open year round. Hours vary with the season, and it's occasionally closed for cleaning, so call ahead.

7 Craters and Freighters.

You can send anything , anywhere in the Austin and San Antonio areas with the expert help of this freight company. From fragile antiques and artwork to household items and heavy equipment, Craters and Freighters knows how to pack and ship items safely and efficiently.

Craters and Freighters start by picking up the item to be shipped at your location. They crate and pack, and then ship it from their base in South Austin. Craters and Freighters staff personally handle your items until their are completely packaged and ready to ship, and their trucks are locked at all times in transit. Packages are insured, tracked, traced and delivered to their destination. It's a hassle-free way to make sure your package gets where it needs to go.

We talked to some Craters and Freighters clients to get their perspective. Wally Workman, owner of Wally Workman Gallery says she once shipped her own art. Not anymore. "Since I discovered Craters and Freighters, I can assure my clients their art purchases will be sent professionally and arrive intact. This is a great relief, and has alleviated our shipping nightmares." Likewise, Mrs. Pace Wilson, owner of Pace Piquante, says the company "has done an outstanding job in handling the packing and shipping of my glass sculpture." And Don Robinson, co-owner of Artworks, calls them reliable, convenient and on the ball. "We love them!" he says.

To call for a quote, please have the origin and destination zip codes available, along with a description of the product, its value and dimensions, and an approximate weight. Many different levels of service are offered, from overnight air to deferred ground.

To find it: 5214 Burleson Road No. 306.
Phone: 512/326-1627, 888/520-1134.
Accepts: Major Credit Cards.
Hours: Mon.-Fri. 9 a.m. to 5 p.m. 24-hour voice mail. Returnable phone calls Saturday 10 a.m. to 2 p.m.
Notable: Specializing in fragile and hard-to-ship items.

Owners Steve Balnis (left) and Kenny Copeland pack furnishings provided by their friends at West End Consignment.

ATTRACTIONS:
The Bremond Block

Forget Southfork, with its Ewing family all crammed into one spacious ranch house. Eugene Bremond had the right idea in 1866 when he bought the north half of a city block in the fledgling city of Austin, envisioning a family compound there.

The merchant banker's vision was strong, and over the years he built homes on the family block for several of his children. His brother also built a beautiful house there. Other prominent Austin citizens filled in with homes of their own, and as the Bremond family grew, it expanded beyond the confines of this block to construct their living quarters in the surrounding neighborhood. Six houses on that original block, plus three across San Antonio Street, became the "family compound" Bremond envisioned. Five other historic homes still stand in the area as well.

The John Bremond House at 706 Guadalupe Street is in the Greek Revival style so popular in the 19th century. Built in 1854 by Abner Cook, the house is the oldest on the block. Eugene Bremond's father, the senior John Bremond, was this house's original owner. Although Eugene eventually moved into this house, he built a frame home for his second wife at 404 West 7th Street in a New Orleans style. This house now is known as the Eugene Bremond House.

Three of the loveliest houses—the Walter Bremond house, which Eugene built as a wedding present for his son; the Pierre Bremond house, another of Eugene's wedding presents; and the John Bremond, Jr. house built by Eugene's brother— are examples of the work of builder George Fiegel, who constructed much of Congress Avenue.

The Walter Bremond House evokes old New Orleans. Built in 1887, the house originally was without its French-Quarter wrought-iron railing; this replaced more Victorian-style fixtures several decades ago.

The John Bremond, Jr. House at 700 Guadalupe was the most expensive house built in Austin at the time. Its mansard roof, fancy ironwork, and ornamental details show why. Besides, it had the city's first indoor toilet. The Pierre Bremond House is less ornate, although still stately and Victorian.

Today, the Bremond Block still stands, a reminder of the life led by Austin's affluent pioneers. Deep in the heart of downtown Austin— between 7th and 8th streets and Guadalupe and San Antonio streets, just blocks from the Capitol—the graceful old homes and shaded streets can take visitors back to a time when the world turned more slowly.

The best way to view the Bremond Block and its environs is on foot, as its residents once did. Park and stroll the neighborhood alone, or, for more information on the individual homes, take a walking tour sponsored by the Austin Convention and Visitors Bureau. The Bremond Block tour is offered weekends at 11 a.m. each day, and lasts about 90 minutes. There is no charge.

For information, call the visitors bureau at 512/478-0098.

Celis Brewery

When Belgian brewer Pierre Celis scoured America for the best possible place to brew his brand of beer, Austin's limestone bluffs, water and proximity to hard wheat won him over. Today, the Celis Brewery is an award-winning producer of specialty brews, including its trademark "white" beer. The story of how Celis and his family came to do so is flavored with the spice of the old country.

Celis grew up in the village of Hoegaarden, Belgium, a town rich in brewing history. As a youngster, Celis worked at the Tomsin Brewery next door to his home, one of 35 different breweries in the village itself. As one could imagine, a town populated by so many breweries housed a populace of beer conoisseurs, many of whom smacked their lips at the thought of the region's trademark white beer, a cloudy potion flavored with spices. The Tomsin brewer told young Pierre never to forget his town's legacy of white beer.

When the small breweries went out of business, white beer went with them, until Pierre Celis decided to bring it back a decade later. He brewed his first batch using a copper washtub and an old stainless steel tank and joked to neighbors that he had some nine- or ten-year-old beer from the Tomsin Brewery. They were delighted to have their traditional beer back. Though his mentor at first looked down his nose at Pierre's first batch, several days later he pronounced it "fit".

Pierre's operation grew over the years until an alliance with a larger brewery went sour. Looking to begin anew, Celis and his daughter, Christine, and son-in-law, Peter Camps, came to Austin with three Belgian copper brewing kettles and built the Celis Brewery.

Celis Brewery produced three kinds of beer initially: White, Pale Bock and Golden. Celis White won a gold metal after the brewery had been operating only six months. The brewery has been winning medals ever since for one type of brew or another; its menu now encompasses seven recipes, including the newly introduced Lagniappe Beer produced from an old New Orleans formula.

Visitors can see Celis' first three copper brewing kettles firsthand during a tour of the local facilities. The rest of the operation literally was built around these kettles, which were the first pieces installed. During the tour, guides also show visitors through the milling room, where the grains used in brewing are ground, and the bottling facility, where the brew is bottled, boxed, and made ready for delivery.

The tours and tastings are complimentary and are conducted Tuesday through Saturday at 2 p.m. and 4 p.m. Fridays, there's an additional tour at 5:30. Tastings are part of the package. One catch: The tour is reserved for those 21 and over. For information, call 512/835-0884.

8   Cherry Creek Catfish Co.

Restaurant owner Shari Braly has cooked up a half-dozen awards for her barbecue, but here in South Austin it's the Southern-style menu she's winning kudos for. The BBQ recipe comes from her general manger Lloyd Helsgen. Headlined by its original crispy fried catfish, Cherry Creek Catfish Co. also serves up shrimp, oysters, chicken-fried steak, burgers, po-boys — not to mention Braly's award-winning ribs and some of the savoriest seafood gumbo in the city.

Add a scrumptious selection of homemade desserts — including the sinfully rich Chocolate Lover's Pie — and you'll leave Cherry Creek with a delightfully full stomach and a sweet smile on your face.

Southern hospitality is not out of style here, either. The smiling staff welcomes diners of all ages, with crayons and special placemats for the kids. Braly works hand-in-hand with her staff and can often be found greeting customers.

Cherry Creek is a great place for a party, too, with a private room seating up to 40. For bigger crowds, the restaurant's catering service offers a host of lunch and dinner entrees, and 16 different side dishes to choose from. Desserts, beverages and appetizers round out the meal to make any celebration a gastronomic delight. Cherry Creek can feed from 50 guests to 2,000, and will even provide specially arranged buffet tables to enhance the theme of your function. Cherry Creek also offers a menu of take-away items; 24 hours' notice is all that's required for groups larger than 50 people.

To find it: 5712 Manchaca, Austin, Texas 78745.
Phone: 512/440-8810.
Accepts: MC, Visa, Amex, Discover.
Hours: 11 a.m. to 9 p.m. Sundays to Thursdays; 11 a.m. to 10 p.m. Fridays and Saturdays.
Notable: Kid-friendly. Great home-baked desserts. Wide selection of menu items, from traditional fried catfish to lighter grilled seafood and chicken. Full-menu catering service highlights award-winning ribs.

Sunflowers on Blue and Red
By Linda Dumont

Sixth Street

Now one of the east-west numbered streets forming the woof of downtown Austin's grid, Sixth Street once was Pecan Street—and Austin's most important commerical strip. Today, after more than 30 years of gentrification, Sixth Street again could be crowned the city's most important thoroughfare.

It's the one most visited by tourists, to be sure. Visitors come by day to shop and stroll through some of the city's oldest buildings. By night, Sixth Street becomes a mecca for college students and other partyers looking to eat, imbibe, dance, and perhaps take in a little of the city's ever-present live music.

Sixth Street so enjoys a party, these days, that there are at least two official—and one unofficial—festivals that shut down the street. The Old Pecan Street Arts Festival celebrates spring and local artists on the first weekend in May, with music, street performers, children's activities, arts and crafts, and of course, food. The spring event is so popular that it now takes place in the fall as well, the last weekend of September.

A few weeks later comes Sixth Street's craziest night of the year, Halloween. Not a festival per se, but certainly an enormous party, complete with the most outrageous costumes imaginable. As many as 60,000 revelers have crammed into the several blocks forming the main Sixth Street party zone, and the celebrating is apt to get out of hand. Needless to say, this isn't a trick-or-treating spot, but for adults only.

To fully appreciate Sixth Street's varied history, take a walking tour. The Austin Convention and Visitors Bureau offers guided walks Thursday through Saturday at 9 a.m. and Sunday at 2 p.m. Or, you can set out on your own, armed with one of the bureau's self-guided booklets. Call 512/478-0098 for more information.

© James Innes

ATTRACTIONS:
SXSW (South by Southwest)

One of the reasons Austin is the music capital of the world is the SXSW Music and Media Conference.

Every spring, SXSW takes over the city. Originally conceived to shine the spotlight on Austin's music scene, SXSW has grown into a triad of conference/festivals on music, film and interactive media. Entertainment folk of all stripes—record producers, musicians, film producers and directors, and agents, just to name a few—descend on Austin from all over the country to schmooze, make deals and have fun.

The film conference and festival, which has been listed as one of the top ten film festivals in the world, kicks off the year 2000 event. SXSW Film presents "the best in new, independent films" and offers film industry types a host of educational opportunities through seminars, panels, workshops and even mentoring sessions. Headlining the 2000 festival is a retrospective of works from Monte Helleman, director of *Two Lane Blacktop*. And, of course, there's a film competition.

Overlapping the film festival's first half is the Interactive Festival, in its seventh year. Multimedia producers and other high-tech professionals will share their expertise and showcase their work. There's also a website competition.

Then, beginning March 15, the Music and Media Conference gets into gear. Keynoted by singer/songwriter Steve Earle, the 2000 event also will host a slate of high-profile music industry speakers. And, of course, more than 800 different musical acts will perform, hoping for their big break—or, for those who already have hit the big time, just to be a part of the spectacle.

SXSW2000 has an extensive web site at sxsw.kdi.com. There, you can register or simply get on the mailing list. Or call 512/467-7979 for info.

Capitol

© James Innes

Texas Capitol Complex

The granite facade of the Texas Capitol towers over downtown Austin in all of its Renaissance Revival glory. Conceived in the early 1880s to replace the much smaller limestone building that had been the original capitol structure, only to burn down after a trash fire got out of control, this state palace ranks as the largest of its kind in all 50 states.

Anyone who has had the chance to walk the long line of portraits of state governors, can appreciate the detailed craftsmanship that went into this grand state house. The portraits stretch all the way to the top of the rotunda, which peaks out at 313 feet, a full six feet taller than the nation's capitol in Washington, D.C.

The state government financed the building with the sale of 3 million acres in the Panhandle, "worthless" property that was disposed of for the nominal rate of 50 cents an acre.

Elijah E. Myers, an architect from Detroit who had already built the Michigan state house and would go on to add the capitol buildings in Colorado and Utah, was picked to design the building. Though state officials chose a slightly scaled down version of his design, they nevertheless managed to impress a state where thinking big was a way of life. Settling on the two big wings that flank the cross-shaped building, granite that was cut and shipped in from Marble Falls to the northwest. Convict labor was used to support the construction, starting with the roads and later for quarrying the granite.

Dedicated in 1888 in a whirlwind of balls and parties, 100 years later the building was in sad shape, suffering from years of neglect and a state economy that was suffering a mighty hangover from the collapse of oil and real estate prices and the demise of its once flourishing savings and loans. But a booming economy in the '90s and a determination to do right by its long, rich history led to a restoration project that stripped away the maze of small offices that had subdivided the capitol into a messy nest.

An underground parking complex and office building was added north of the Capitol, housing a large portion of the Legislature and connected by a series of tunnels. Underground areas are brilliantly lit, almost as if the full powers of the sun were shining inside. Five years and $187 million later, the restoration and expansion was complete, and hailed in another round of Texas-sized celebrations.

Both House and Senate chambers were restored to look like they did 90 years ago, and you can see for yourself as both areas are opened to the public when the Legislature is not in session. Portraits of famous Texans line the chambers' walls.

For those curious to see Texas politics in action, third floor galleries look out over the House and Senate. Visitors, though, are required to keep their seats while in the galleries.

Outside, you'll find beautiful, wide open spaces, dotted with more than 25 species of native trees-- including a few fine examples of Texas' state tree, the pecan. Don't forget to check out the Tyler rose garden, which you'll find on the northwest side of the grounds.

Town Lake

© James Inne

© James Innes

© James Innes

ATTRACTIONS:
Lake Travis

One of seven sparkling jewels in the chain of Highland Lakes, Lake Travis is the largest and the longest of its sisters. It's also the most popular for recreation. The promise of fishing, boating, scuba diving, and sailing brings thousands of visitors to Lake Travis each year. Not to mention the fact that its shoreline is coveted real estate.

Not bad for a lake created in 1941 to help control flooding along the Colorado River. Lake Travis was formed when Mansfield Dam was built, a 266-foot-high and 7,089-foot-long regulator of the river's flow. Today it is the most important of the Highland lakes in controlling flooding that, before the dams, ravaged Central Texas on a fairly regular basis. Lake Travis's level fluctuates as the need arises; it has climbed as high as 707 feet above sea level (its spillway tops out at 714 feet) and has sunk as low at 614 feet.

If you're not lucky enough to own a piece of Lake Travis shoreline—and your own dock—there are plenty of spots where you can enjoy the scenery and enjoy whichever water sports your heart desires. At least 17 public parks and one private park offer entree to the water. Many charge admission; if you're a regular, it makes sense to purchase annual permits. Some of the parks offer overnight camping; some don't allow motorized boats. Information about the individual parks can be had by calling Travis County at 512/473-9437.

A discussion of Lake Travis wouldn't be complete without a mention of Hippie Hollow (MacGregor Park), an Austin institution. This is the infamous nude-bathing beach, which attracts both skinnydippers and nosy observers. The view of the lake and shore, is eye-pleasing. You must be 18 or older to enter, and there's a per-vehicle charge.

99

© James Innes

ATTRACTIONS:

University of Texas Tower

It's one of the most recognizable—and notorious—sights in Austin.

The University of Texas Tower, long one of the tallest structures in the city, is also one of its trademarks. Lit at night, the Tower is a grand site, and when the light glows orange, that means the Texas Longhorns have won a game and the campus is celebrating.

Built in the 1930s and designed by architect Paul Cret, the 307-foot Tower houses UT's administration. The bell tower on top has a three-and-one-half-ton bell that strikes the hours, along with a 56-bell Knicker Carillon that plays on the quarter hour. Around the bell tower is an observation deck that for years was a great spot to take in a panoramic view of Austin.

But all that changed in the late sixties and early seventies. As most of the world knows, the Tower was the site of the Charles Whitman sniper shootings, which left 17 dead. The observation deck was closed for some time afterward, but then reopened, only to play host to a series of suicides. It was closed indefinitely in 1975.

Indefinitely ended in Fall 1999. The University's new president, Larry Faulkner, persuaded its Board of Regents to reopen the observation deck—after certain precautions

© James Innes

were taken. A steel safety barrier was installed to protect people who might think of jumping. To prevent a shooting, visitors are allowed to carry only cameras, binoculars, and purses up to the deck, and police escort them to and fro.

In August 1999, on the 33rd anniversary of the shootings, a garden memorial to the sniper's victims was dedicated by university officials. Created in 1934 as a botanical garden and known by students as the "turtle pond" because of a pool along one side, the half-acre plot is now dubbed Tower Garden.

101

Austin's Best is pleased to announce that a percentage of the proceeds from each book sale will benefit Safeplace and Travis County Children's Advocacy Center.

Throughout the year Austin's Best will also host events that will benefit these charities.

For upcoming events contact High Mountain Publishing
(512) 345-9804

SafePlace. For many families suffering under domestic violence or reeling from the impact of incest or sexual abuse, the darkness surrounding them seems impenetrable. They see no way out. They desperately need a ray of hope.

SafePlace exists to provide that light in the darkness. Created in 1998 by the union of The Center for Battered Women and the Austin Rape Crisis Center, SafePlace now offers help and support to survivors of domestic violence, sexual abuse and incest—and works to end this abuse through education and other outreach programs.

With 24-hour hotlines for victims of domestic violence and sexual abuse, SafePlace stands ready, day or night, to help. The organization offers emergency shelter to those fleeing abusive situations, and supportive housing as they gain independence. They are provided with home furnishings, clothing, and household essentials through SafePlace ThriftPlace, which collects donations of these items and sells those not used by SafePlace clients.

SafePlace provides counseling, care and support to alleviate initial

"I had hit rock bottom ... and it was a long, hard road back. But now ... I know where I'm going."
SafePlace client

"You have given me the insight and the courage to help myself and my children to a safer, better life."
SafePlace client

trauma and put victims on the road to recovery. And it helps families navigate the halls of bureaucracy and the courts as they work to change their lives.

At the same time, SafePlace reaches out to the community to try to prevent the violence and abuse that is so pervasive in our society today. They sponsor educational programs—such as Expect Respect, which aims to show teenagers how to recognize abuse and how to escape it—that reach thousands of Austin-area students. They offer domestic violence training to people with disabilities and their families and caregivers. And through several high-profile fundraising events—including a Valentine's Gala and the Walk for Safe Families & Safe Streets—SafePlace increases community awareness of these problems while raising money to support its activities.

SafePlace needs help, from volunteers who want to give their time and from individuals and companies that want to contribute funds. For more information about how to get involved in the fight against domestic violence and sexual assault or abuse, call SafePlace's Resource Center listed below.

Mailing Address: P.O. Box 19454, Austin, Texas 78760.
SafePlace ThriftPlace: 4631 Airport Blvd., 512/451-4108.
Resource Center Phone: 512/385-5181 (voice), 482-0691 (TDD).
24-hour Domestic Violence Hotline: 512/928-9070 (voice, TDD).
24-hour Sexual Assault Hotline: 512/440-7273 (voice), 440-7363 (TDD).
Online: www.austin-safeplace.org
Notable: Serves victims of domestic violence and sexual abuse and their families, reaching thousands across the city each year.

Westlake & Lakeway

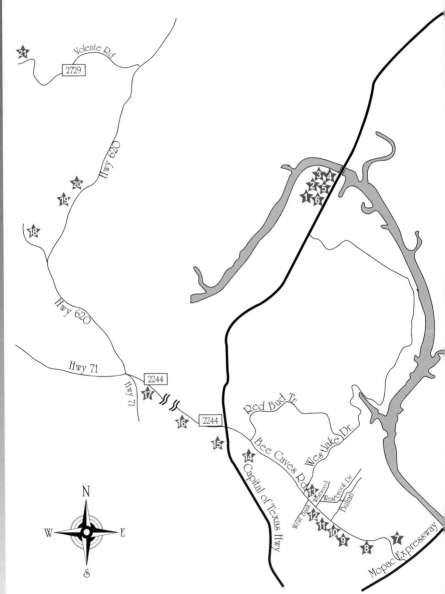

Volente Rd

2729

Hwy 620

Hwy 620

Hwy 71

Hwy 71

2244

2244

Red Bud Tr.

Bee Caves Rd.

Westlake Dr.

Capital of Texas Hwy

West Brook Dr.

Dullan

Mopac Expressway

N
W   E
S

Call this Austin's land of the lakes. Every weekend when the weather is good, Austinites flock to Lake Travis and Lake Austin for water sports, or just to dine or relax at one of the restaurants with a view. Golfers come, too, to play their trade at one of the many courses nearby. If playing in or by the lake isn't your idea of fun, it's worth the drive here just to gaze at the huge, beautiful houses and browse the eclectic shops.

13 Austin Presence.

Owners Ted Hayes and Bruce MacKenzie-Graham are purveyors of fine things. Fine art, certainly, as a glance at the walls of their shop will attest. But also fine crystal, fine silks, fine leather — even the finest in bath salts.

When the two men set out to open their shop, they decided they would only carry the best — the very best — in any category they decided

to stock. When they decided to sell candles, they found a source that offers dining tapers in six sizes. When they wanted to offer men's wallets, they found a vendor with the softest, butteriest leather you've ever felt in a billfold — and it wears like iron.

So it goes throughout Austin Presence. Every item one examines is well-made of wonderfully luxurious materials. They all show an attention to good design. And the art objects— from art glass to hand-painted scarves to sculpture and paintings— are not only beautiful, but unusual. You won't find these artists displayed in any old upscale department store.

The philosophy of simply offering wonderful things pays off for those searching for a hard-to-find gift — or a present for oneself. A stroll through Austin Presence yields gift ideas galore. But if you're still stumped, one of the owners is always on hand to assist, and because of their exhaustive research on each line in the shop, they know how to help. Extras such as gift wrap and shipping are handled with ease, and delicate, hard-to-ship items are handled with extreme care. Become a regular customer, and Ted or Bruce will even call you when something arrives that matches your taste. Or, if your significant other wants to buy you that fragrance you are addicted to, they'll look you up on the computer to check your preferences.

Such attention to detail and meticulous service makes shopping at Austin Presence a pleasure worth repeating. It's clear that the owners love their store and everything in it. And they have such good taste, you'll love it, too!

To find it: 3736 Bee Caves Road, Austin, Texas 78746.
Phone: 512/306-9636.
Fax: 512/306-9637.
Accepts: MC, Visa, Amex, personal checks.
Hours: 10 a.m. to 6 p.m. Tuesdays to Fridays, 10 a.m. to 4 p.m. Saturdays, closed Sundays and Mondays.
Shipping: Available at cost.
Notable: Local artists' work shown here. Fine collection of unusual art glass. Wonderful leather goods. Gifts of all kinds, for all people.

18 Sterling Affairs. Austin's only true full-service event production company melds experience and creativity to create events so unique, dramatic and memorable, they'll exceed your wildest dreams.

Sterling Affairs began in 1995 as the brainchild of Jan Brainard and Larry Kille (pictured at right); now it's one of the top three event planning and catering companies, according to the *Austin Business Journal*. The company's growth earned it a nomination for the prestigious Entrepreneur of the Year award in 1999.

Sterling Affairs has grown quickly by applying the experience and originality of its staff to take each event beyond the expected. Besides Jan and Larry, who have a combined 50 years experience in all areas of special event planning, Sterling Affairs boasts a staff of more than 65, including eight of the city's most creative chefs and 15 very experienced event managers. They all work together to produce taste-tempting menus and a beautiful environment for enjoying them. But Sterling Affairs doesn't stop there. The company adds music, lighting, dance and special effects to make each event unforgettable. Perhaps that's why Dell Computer Corp.

chose Sterling Affairs as its outstanding vendor for 1999.

Sterling Affairs also offers facilties on Lake Travis and in Lakeway to provide a stunning backdrop for parties and weddings. The Vintage Villas Wedding Center, Pyramid on Lake Travis and World of Tennis in

Lakeway all have custom facilities for all sizes of meetings, receptions and special events.

To find it: One World of Tennis Square.
Phone: 512/261-0142.
Fax: 512/261-2286.
Online: www.sterlingaffairs.com
Email: sa@inetport.com
Accepts: Visa & MC.
Hours: 8:30 to 6p.m. M-F, 10-2 Sat.
Notable: Austin's only full-service catering, event planning, productions and rental company. Special Events and Wedding Centers on Lake Travis and in Lakeway.

7 Abercrombie Jewelry.

This family-owned and - operated store keeps alive the tradition of personal, people-oriented service for those seeking jewelry and fine china, crystal and silver.

The Rosenberg family searches far and wide for the best in vintage jewelry and watches, and their selection is amazing. Pre-owned watches include Patek Phillipe and Rolex; new watches are also available. Loose diamonds are sold at 10 percent over wholesale cost. Pre-owned fine china, crystal and silver, from names such as Lalique and Steuben often can be found here as well.

As a service to customers, the shop maintains a full repair facility, with a jeweler and watch repairman on premises. They'll even do custom designs.

To find it: 3010 Bee Caves Road, Suite 100, Austin, 78746.
Phone: 512/328-7530.
Accepts: MC, Visa, Amex. Personal checks.
Hours: Monday-Friday 9 a.m. to 5:30 p.m., Saturday 9 a.m. to 1 p.m.
Notable: Vintage jewelry. Personal service. New and pre-owned fine watches.

8 C~D~C Carpets & Interiors.

The best in carpet and flooring can be found at this shop, but that's not all. In-house designers can consult on all aspects of interior finish, including window treatments and fabrics, making C~D~C a must for anyone building a new home.

The selection here is exclusive and broad. Offerings include wool carpets not available anywhere else in Austin, Seagrass, sisal and other natural floor coverings. Brands such as Schumacher, Stanton, Wilton Gallery Collections.

Besides the wonderful products, C~D~C's staff makes big decisions easier with their knowledge and experience. Samples are available to try your selection at home, and C~D~C's installers are top-notch.

To find it: 3425 Bee Caves Road, Austin, 78746.
Phone: 512/327-8326.
Accepts: MC, Visa, Amex. Personal checks.
Hours: Monday-Friday, 9 a.m. to 5 p.m.
Notable: Best selection of wool carpet . Natural floorings such as sisal and cork. Custom rugs and window treatments.

14 Furniture Brokers of Westlake.

This upscale consignment store offers Henredon, Drexel, Thomasville and Roche-BoBois. In addition to these fine furnishings, they carry Waterford crystal, Wedgwood china and an array of exceptional accessories.

Furniture Brokers, a woman-owned and -operated business, offers a carefully selected array of furniture, artwork, floral arrangements and collectors' items, all at consignment-store prices. This is a store to visit often, because new inventory arrives almost daily. Each piece eligible for consignment is carefully previewed to make sure everything in the 4,000-square-foot showroom is in nearly new condition.

In addition to the great finds here, the store's trained and friendly staff is ready to answer any questions and will even give decorating advice.

To find it: 4201 Westbank Drive, Austin, Texas 78746.
Phone: 512/329-8421.
Accepts: MC, Visa, Discover, Personal checks.
Hours: Monday-Friday, 10 a.m. to 6 p.m. Saturdays 9:30 a.m. to 5 p.m.
Notable: Will consult with clients on home design. Well-known and exclusive brands of furniture and accessories.

James M. Innes. For this photographer, every day is an adventure. The joy and passion of his life has been capturing the images of many special places. He has photographed extensively in Austin, Europe, Great Britain, Israel, the Virgin Islands, Colorado, California, New York, Texas, New Mexico, and many other places.

Innes' work is featured throughout *Austin's Best*. It also has been featured in the following books: *Austin: Lone Star Rising*, *Austin: Celebrating the New Millennium*, and *Austin: A Historical Portrait*.

Since December of 1989, Innes has photographed more than 1,200 commercial real estate projects. He has shot interiors, exteriors and even aerials of these projects.

He also has hundreds of images of Austin, including aerial views. Some of these images show Austin as it appeared on January 1, 2000. They include shots of the skyline, of the State Capitol, of the State Highway 360 Bridge, and more.

Innes also has the Austin at Twilight poster and the Austin 2000 Calendar available in local retail stores.

For more information or to view the photographer's images, visit the two websites below. Or contact him via email or telephone.

Phone: 512/327-5277.
Online: www.jamesminnes.com, www.austinimages.com
Email: innes@io.com
Notable: Hundreds of Austin images. His work has appeared in three books, and on posters and calendars.

10 Barton Springs Nursery.

Since 1986, owners Conrad and Bernadine Bering have taken pride in offering one of the best selections of native plants in Central Texas. The majority of their plants grow on-site in the nursery, where they become acclimated to the soil, water and climate. When you buy a plant here, it already knows Central Texas is home, and it's more likely to make an easy transition to your landscape. They also cultivate unusual plants so they, too, can take root in the Central Texas soil. If you're looking for something new to jazz up the garden, this is the right place.

The Berings also are committed to progressive horticulture and responsible gardening. They offer products for environmentally friendly pest management, organic techniques and water conservation.

Take a stroll around the three-and-a-half acre spread, and you'll see an amazing array of plants that can transform your outdoor space: perennials, annuals, herbs, ornamental grasses, ground covers, native shrubs and trees, waterlilies, bog plants, tropical plants and cacti. The nursery also boasts one of the largest selections of antique roses and salvias in the area. Among the plants are all the accessories you need to make your garden extraordinary, from tools and fertilizers to fountains and lanterns. A grove of live oak trees provides a natural spot for shade-loving plants, as well as a quiet place to rest and think about how your landscape can speak best to you. If the kids are along, they'll love the sandbox play space and the parrots and doves that roost in the aviary.

The Berings and their knowledgeable staff are on hand to answer your questions and direct you to informational resources if you're interested. If there's an item you need that isn't on hand, make a request and they will do their best to find it for you. They also maintain a list of designers who can help you re-envision your own slice of Texas.

So stop by and experience first-hand some of the enchantment sprouting from the land at Barton Springs Nursery.

To find it: 3601 Bee Caves Road.
Phone: 512/328-6655.
Accepts: MC, Visa, Amex, Discover and personal checks.
Hours: 9 a.m. to 6 p.m. Mondays to Saturdays, 10 a.m. to 6 p.m. Sundays. Closed only on Christmas, Thanksgiving and New Year's Day.
Notable: Native plants and those well-adapted to the Central Texas climate. Knowledgable staff. Advocates progressive, responsible gardening.

9 **Westbank Flower Market.**
Westbank Flower Market isn't just a florist — it's a gift shop, flower market, and design studio, all in one.

Stop by to browse for a gift or for something to brighten up the home. You'll find earthy treasures, including dried and freeze-dried flowers and fruit. Arrange your newly found riches in one of the beautiful containers here, from Indian turned wood vessels to Asian porcelain to silver or crystal. Or pick up Mexican church candles , fragrant sachets or handmade papers instead.

Of course, living flowers and plants can be had, including potted orchids and tropical house plants.

For special occasions, such as weddings, Westbank Flower Market uses the best imported flowers. Unusual candelabra, silver epergnes, urns and pedastals serve as foundations for their one-of-a-kind designs. To ensure that their work fits your vision for that special occasion, Westbank staff will even come to your home for a free consultation.

To find it: 3535 Bee Caves Road.
Phone: 512/327-2552.
Accepts: Major credit cards, checks.
Hours: Mondays-Fridays 8:30 a.m. to 5:30 p.m. Saturdays 10 a.m. to 5 p.m.
Notable: Home consultation for custom work. Unusual vases, containers.

11 **Elle Boutique.** The feeling in Elle Boutique is of relaxed elegance, and that extends to the merchandise. Owner Nicole Nutt believes in unique, feminine

clothes with classic lines, fashioned of the finest materials. Her collection of ladies' apparel covers a wide variety of activewear to after-five options, at a wide range of prices. It also encompasses accessories from jewelry to handbags and hats. Featured brands include Joseph A, Victoria Pappas and Finley, and some jewelry is made by local artists.

Elle is also committed to service with a personal touch. There's even a seating area with a television and magazines to entertain husbands, as well as toys for the children. So shopping at Elle is not just tasteful and enjoyable, it's convenient.

To find it: 3663 Bee Caves Road, Austin, Texas, 78746.
Phone: 512/327-2552.
Accepts: MC, Visa, Amex. Personal checks with a Central Texas address.
Hours: Mondays-Thursdays 10 a.m. to 7 p.m. Fridays-Saturdays 10 a.m. to 6 p.m. Closed Sundays, New Year's Day, Fourth of July, Thanksgiving and Christmas.
Notable: Free gift wrap. Distinctive ceiling mural. Nice collection of evening wear, petite clothing.

12 Quality Frames ... & Art.

There's no better place to go in Austin for custom picture framing and art than this fine shop. The quality of the work here is incredible — so good that it took second place nationwide in a competition sponsored by the Professional Picture Framers Association of America.

The selection of materials is wonderful, including a full line of Larson Juhl mouldings, which have been featured in *Architectural Digest* and other national magazines. The staff works closely with interior designers and will even visit your home for a consultation. If you need something finished quickly, there's one-day service on in-stock orders.

Quality Frames will showcase your needlework, create a shadowbox for treasured objects, or custom-design a mirror. Frames can be repaired and glass replaced.

And if you're looking for the art itself, browse through the on-site gallery. Simply called & Art, it features a wide selection of oils, water-colors and bronzes from local and regional artists. Jack Terry, Peggy Byars, Joy Harris, Nina Mihm, John Scanlan and many others have their work shown here. It's an array of affordable, fine art that meets any need or taste. And if you have any doubt about a particular piece, you can take it home to make sure you like it, under the shop's "take-it-home" proof service.

As you can see, Quality Frames ... & Art offers one-stop shopping for all your custom picture-framing and art needs. They can even deliver and install the artwork for you. All you have to do is enjoy.

To find it: 3663 Bee Caves Road, Suite 4E. Austin, Texas 78746.
Phone: 512/328-3631.
Fax: 512/328-3642.
Accepts: MC, Visa, Amex, Discover.
Hours: 9:30 a.m. to 6 p.m. Mondays to Fridays; 9:30 a.m. to 4 p.m. Saturdays.
Notable: Nationally award-winning member of Professional Picture Framers Association of America. One-day service for in-stock orders.

Lake Travis

© James Innes

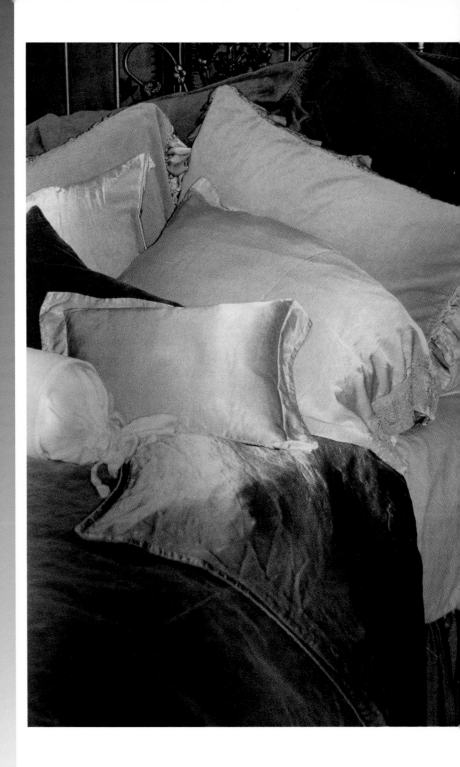

15 **La Provence.** The scent of lavender in the air is a fitting introduction to this shop, named after the region in France where the herb is grown by fields-

full. Indeed, the owners of La Provence grew tired of lugging suitcases full of European-style soaps and bath products back from the continent, so they decided to bring these goods to Austin. To this core of pampering items, they've added luxury bed and bath linens for adults and wee ones, including a fabulous line of crib bedding and nursery accessories. We guarantee that after browsing around, you'll want to curl up in one of these sumptuous beds, preferably with a lavender-scented candle burning nearby.

To find it: 701 Capitol of Texas Hwy. S., Suite F610, Westlake Hills.
Phone: 512/347-7939.
Accepts: MC, Visa, Amex, Discover. Personal checks with ID.
Hours: Mon.-Sat. 10 a.m. to 6 p.m.
Notable: Luxury linens, bed and bath. Special-order, custom furniture. Stylish baby clothes.

16 **County Line Restaurants.** Both County Line locations serve excellent barbecue —from ribs to brisket to chicken and more — in a fun atmosphere reminiscent of a Texas roadhouse.

County Line on the Hill. Located in a historic rock building perched on one of the highest hills in the area, this County Line offers a 20-mile view of the Texas Hill country. The sunsets are spectacular, and so is the food, including a full line of grilled items such as steak, fish and kabobs.

To find it: 6500 W. Bee Caves Road.
Phone: 512/327-1742.
Accepts: All major credit cards.
Hours: Dinner only, seven days a week.
Notable: Entire restaurant may be reserved for private luncheons, seven days a week.

County Line on the Lake. Set in an old lake lodge, this County Line is

right on the water. Cocktails on the lower deck are a must, and the lower dining area has five huge windows overlooking the deck and lake. Specialties include smoked prime rib and smoked pork tenderloin.

To find it: 5204 F.M. 2222.
Phone: 512/346-3664.
Accepts: All major credit cards.
Hours: Lunch and dinner, seven days a week.
Notable: Accessible by boat. Private party room seats 20-60.

6 **Davenport Village** This Capital of Texas Highway shopping center is a haven for upscale shopping and great dining.

2 **Copeland Jewelers:** A fixture on the Austin jewelry scene since 1983, this jewelry store and repair center recently moved to Davenport Village. In the new location, Copeland Jewelers is still a mainstay of personal, attentive service and fine jewelry design. Besides custom work, the shop carries such names as John Atencio, Bagley & Hotchkiss, Maurice Lacroix, Cyma and Hamilton. Diamonds are available, of course, as are colored gems. Copeland's also offers watch repair and jewelry appraisals. No wonder owner Clay Copeland says the shop specializes in customer service.

To find it: 3801 Capital of Texas Highway, Suit D160. Austin, Texas 78746.
Phone: 512/330-0303.
Accepts: MC, Visa, Discover. Personal checks with ID.
Hours: 10 a.m. to 6 p.m. Monday to Wednesday; 10 a.m. to 7 p.m. Thursday; 10 a.m. to 6 p.m. Friday; 10 a.m. to 5 p.m. Saturday.

4 **Thistle Cafe:** The heavenly smells that greet customers at this American-style bistro are reason enough to stop by. We guarantee you'll stay for a taste. The Thistle serves high-quality food fashioned from fresh ingredients in an atmosphere that is casual and fun, yet ele-gant. Take-out food is available breakfast, lunch and dinner, and picnic baskets can even be stocked here. Make sure to include some of the delectable cookies and other desserts! Lunch is served on weekdays, dinner Monday through Saturday nights, and brunch on Sunday. Breakfast is served on Saturday as well. Catering services are available for all occasions.

To find it: 3801 Capital of Texas Highway, Suite C200, Austin, Texas 78746.
Phone: 512/347-1000.
Accepts: MC, Visa, Amex,Diners
Hours: 9 a.m. to 9 p.m. Monday through Thursday; 9 a.m. to 9:30 p.m. Friday. 8 a.m. to 9:30 p.m. Saturday. 8 a.m. to 3 p.m. Sunday.

Studio 29: This European hair salon and day spa is the kingdom of the Mueller family and has roots that are 80 years old. Started in Germany in 1919 by Grandpapa Heinrich Mueller, who worked at home with one barber chair, the family tradition now is carried on by Norbert and Petra Mueller in Austin. They have expanded far beyond the one chair to offer a complete selection of spa services, including massage, steam therapy, manicures, pedicures and, of course, hair care. They offer hair products from Graham Webb, Matrix, Alterna and Goldwell, a German line. Skin care products are from Pevonia.

To find it: 3801 Capital of Texas Highway N., Suite E200.
Phone: 512/328-4342.
Accepts: Visa, MC, Amex, local personal checks.
Hours: 9 a.m. to 7 p.m. Mondays, Tuesdays, Wednesdays, Fridays; 9 a.m. to 8 p.m. Thursdays; 9 a.m. to 5 p.m. Saturdays.

3 **We-B-Toys.** This specialty toy store's motto is "Where Education and Fun Connect." A perusal of the shelves inside shows what they mean: Quality toys that kids love, all with an eye toward developing a child's mind and imagination.

Just a sampling of the wonderful items available here: Madame Alexander dolls, Thomas the Train and Brio train sets, Peg Perego toys and vehicles, Lamaze developmental playthings for babies and toddlers, Corolle dolls, Playmobil play sets, and Breyer horses and play sets.

All kids love to go to toy stores, but We-B-Toys is especially fun. Two wooden train sets stand just inside the door, waiting for little hands to put them to use. The friendly, staff lets children test the toys (within reason!), eliminating guesswork. And they're always ready with answers and suggestions for adults overwhelmed by the wonderful choices.

To find it: 3801 Capital of Texas Highway, Suit D180. Austin, Texas 78746.
Phone: 512/306-9255.
Accepts: MC, Visa, Discover, Amex. Personal checks with ID.
Hours: 10 a.m. to 6 p.m. Mondays to Saturdays; extended holiday hours.

5 **Pacifica.** Step into this restaurant and find yourself in the tropics. The atmosphere evokes a British Colonial plantation on a South Sea island, and the glittering cuisine presented on crisp white table linens brings that region's flavor to life.

Under specially crafted stained-glass light fixtures, you can sample the exquisite menu of Chef Michael Neff, featuring fresh seafood as well as beef, pork, chicken and vegetarian dishes, while gazing out the huge, custom windows. Presented with panache, everything from appetizer to dessert reflects the vibrant tastes of the Pacific, the most sophisticated culinary landscape in the world. Desserts vary daily, but usually include cheesecake, sorbets and assorted chocolate delicacies.

Pacifica's concierge service hosts special events, including such unique packages as a dinner-theater evening. The restaurant's private room seats 40, and the entire place can be reserved for up to 250.

To find it: 3801 Capital of Texas Highway, Suite A180. Austin, Texas 78746.
Phone: 512/327-3332.
Fax: 512/327-5528.
Accepts: MC, Visa, Amex, Diners, Discover.
Hours: 11:30 a.m. to 2 p.m. Monday-Friday; 5:30-10 p.m. Monday-Thursday; 5:30-11pm Friday-Saturday; 10:30 a.m. to 2 p.m. Sunday.

20 **Suzie D's** Shop at this Lakeway boutique and you'll always have a distinctive look. Owner Sue DeBree offers clothing lines not found in department stores, and she buys in small quantities to keep her customers' look unique. The look is contemporary, casual, one-of-a-kind, in wonderful fabrics. Her fashion lines include Tommy Bahama, Cosabella, VIVYD, Cyrus and Mill Valley Cotton. Some of the pieces have distinctive detailing; others are simply striking. Suzie D's also offers accessories such as scarves, jewelry and belts to add an extra touch to any outfit. And while you're adding to your wardrobe, you can also shop for gifts for any occasion. — Sue's wonderful taste extends to her collection of gifts!

To find it: 900 Ranch Road, 620 South, Suite A103, Austin, Texas, 78734.
Phone: 512/263-0329.
Accepts: MC, Visa, Amex, Discover. Personal checks.
Hours: Mondays-Fridays 10 a.m. to 6 p.m. ; Saturdays 10 a.m. to 5 p.m.
Notable: Free gift packaging. Distinctive selection of clothing. Great fabrics for local climate.

19 **LadyBugs Cards and Gifts.** You may feel as if you're stepping back into your childhood when you venture into this gift and card shop in Lakeway. Beautiful, collectible dolls and figurines line the shelves along with stuffed animals, music boxes and a wide variety of

greeting cards. Candles, pottery and bath products round out the selection of gifts, ensuring that something for everyone can be found here. Among the special items are Reuge Music Boxes, Russ Vintage Bears, M.I. Hummel figurines, Precious Moments Dolls, special one-of-a-kind porcelain dolls by Sheila Rhodes and Lee Middleton dolls, Honeybourne Hollow Bear. The pack-and-mail center next door, under the same ownership as LadyBugs, makes it convenient to buy a wonderful gift and ship it anywhere in the world.

To find it: In Lakeway Commons, 900 R.R. 620 South, Suite C102, Lakeway.
Phone: 512/263-7227.
Email: krmoody@flash.net
Accepts: MC, Visa, Amex, Discover. Personal checks.
Hours: Monday-Friday, 9:30 a.m. to 6:30 p.m.; Saturday 10 a.m. to 5 p.m.
Notable: Limited edition dolls; collectible figurines and teddy bears.

17 **Cowgirls are Forever.**
For fashion with a Western accent, there's no better place than this rustic-but-sophisticated bou-

tique. Housed in a log-cabin-style building, Cowgirls are Forever offers classic Texan and sophisticated Western attire from such names as Double D Ranchwear, The Manuel Collection, Painted Pony, Stubbs Collection, and its own signature leather and suede line, S.H.E. You can either buy a few pieces to spice up your existing wardrobe — many of the jackets, for example, are easy to mix and match — or go all out with complete outfits, hats, boots, jewelry and belts. The shop even carries attire for the serious cowgirl: vests and jackets to wear in the Western show ring. Whether you're serious or not, though, Cowgirls are Forever can be that "something different" that your closet needs.

To find it: 12500 Bee Caves Road, Austin, Texas 78733.
Phone: 512/263-7009.
Accepts: MC, Visa, Amex, Discover. Personal checks.
Hours: Tuesday-Saturday 10 a.m. to 6 p.m. ; except Thursday 10 a.m. to 7 p.m.
Notable: Exclusive suede and leather line, S.H.E. Free alterations on purchases over $150.

21 **Utopia.** For cruising Lake Travis in style, call Mitch and Louise Phillips. The couple offers first-class charters aboard the Utopia, a 78-foot luxury yacht with four bedrooms and two baths. It's fully equipped for a big party or an intimate, relaxing cruise. Whether it's chartered for a business meeting, office party, birthday, wedding, or simply having fun with friends, the Phillipses are on hand to take the burden off the host so everyone can enjoy themselves.

Just a glance at Utopia's specifications shows the abundance of amenities available. The yacht is equipped with every kitchen appliance, large and small, including two ice makers, crock pots, even dishes and flatware. The salon features leather recliners, a sumptuous sleeper sofa and a top-of-the-line sound system with speakers and volume controls on every deck — so you'll never be without your favorite tunes for dancing. You can bring your own music selection or choose from the broad collection available on board.

On the upper deck, there's a propane grill for cooking, a three-person waverunner available to rent, and a large hot tub with seating for six. The rear deck has access to the water for swimming.

If weather permits use of all the decks, the Utopia can accommodate up to 60 people. If inclement weather restricts activities to indoors, up to 30 can enjoy the comforts of this spacious yacht.

So, if you want to host an event to impress, call early to ensure your prefered date. With this yacht, you can truly find Utopia.

To find it: VIP Marina at Volente Beach, Lake Travis.
Mailing Address: 15971 Booth Circle, Leander, Texas 78641.
Phone: 512/918-0931.
Online: www.utopiancruises.com
Email: utopia@utopiancruises.com
Accepts: Cash, personal checks up to 21 days before the event.
Hours: 8 a.m. to 9 p.m. daily. Open holidays.
Notable: Personal attention from boat owners. Beautiful, luxury yacht. Room for up to 60 people.

Lake Travis   © James Innes

ΛTTRΛCTIONS:
Lake Austin

Water skiing devotees should make a point of spending at least one day indulging their favorite sport at beautiful Lake Austin.

The scenery here is unparallelled, and it's also a great place for a picnic, playing, swimming, or hiking.

Seven public parks and several boat ramps ring the lakeshore. Among these are the lake at the Loop 360 Boat Ramp at 5020 Capital of Texas Highway and Mary Quinlan Park's ramp on the lake at the end of Quinlan Park Road. Both are available free of charge. For a fee, you can use the facilities at Emma Long Metropolitan Park, one of the city's biggest and most historic parks. Also called City Park, it has several boat ramps and a hiking trail with fine views of the lake from 1,000-foot-cliffs. So even if you're just along for the ride, City Park's high elevation makes it possible to watch the local water sports from a terrific vantage spot.

Fritz Hughes Park has 5 acres covered with playgrounds, tennis courts and clean restrooms. If you're looking for more room to roam, try Commons Ford Metropolitan Park, which covers 215 acres. Day permits cost $5 per vehicle.

Whether you're new to waterskiing or a seasoned expert, you may want to check out the city's two ski clubs. The Austin Ski Club and the Capital Area Ski Club both offer tournaments throughout the year, and coaching and clinics are available for enthusiasts to hone their skills.

121

© James Innes

Red Sail on Travis
By Linda Dumont

124

A night on the town in Austin can take on as many different personalities as you like. Dinner out could be family style, in a kid-friendly restaurant. Then again, it could be a romantic affair, with white linens and candlelight and innovative cuisine. Afterwards, you could take in live music at a club or slip into a theater or music hall for a performance. Or simply having cocktails by the lake while the sun sets—that's always a pleasing possibility.

ZACHARY SCOTT THEATRE CENTER "BEST THEATRE COMPANY!"

"**ZACH scores again thanks to its mix of stylish, toe-tappin' musicals and beautifully realized plays. Our readers know that whatever the fare, the show will be carefully conceived and professionally executed at every level!**" – *The Austin Chronicle, '99 Best of Austin issue.*

Beehive, 1998-99 Season. Photos by: Kirk R. Tuck

With lustrous sets, dizzying choreography and critically acclaimed performances, Zachary Scott Theatre Center (ZACH), delivers spectacle with captivating craft, time and time again. Founded in 1933, ZACH is Austin's oldest, producing live theatre company. Each new season offers a wide range of entertainment including contemporary musicals, come-

The Mystery of Irma Vep. 1998-99 Season

dies, classic plays and holiday spectaculars. Recent and upcoming productions include: **The Rocky Horror Show, Angels in America, Love, Janis and Tapestry: The Music of Carol King.** With the reputation for "Best Razzle Dazzle" ZACH's powerhouse productions play annually to over 150,000 patrons. ZACH engages the imaginations of its audience with productions that reflect the vitality of Central Texas, making it one the most popular and unique theatres in the Southwest.

ZACH produces its season on two stages centrally located on scenic Town Lake: The Kleberg Stage, W. Riverside at S. Lamar, and the adjacent John R. Whisenhunt Arena Stage at 1510 Toomey Rd. ZACH also offers a performing arts school for children, teens and adults, and Project InterAct a touring, professional youth program to area schools.

To Find It: 1510 Toomey Road, (corner of Riverside Dr. & S. Lamar) Austin, TX 78704.
Administration: 512/476-0594
Box Office: 512/476-0541, ext: 1
Email: info@zachscott.com
Web: www.zachscott.com
Accepts: MC, Visa, AMEX, Discover, and Personal Checks.
Box Office Hours: 12 noon – 7 p.m., Monday – Saturday & 12 - 3 p.m., Sunday.
Notable: ZACH offers high quality, live productions year around on two stages.

Austin Symphony Orchestra.

The city's oldest performing arts group, the Austin Symphony offers an extensive repertoire of an orchestra's bread and butter: classical music. But ASO also reaches out to the young through Young People's Concerts and Family Concerts, and presents a lighthearted series of Pops Concerts each year.

Led by conductor Peter Bay, the Classical series of eight concert pairs runs monthly, September through April, in Bass Concert Hall. The 2000 series includes Beethoven's "Dream Team," the Eroica Trio; Verdi's *Requiem* as sung by the Austin Civic Chorus; and violinist Pamela Frank playing Vivaldi, Dvorak and Respighi. The Pops Concerts are held at Palmer Auditorium, where audiences bring picnic dinners to spread at their tables. This season's Family Concerts include a multicultural musical adventure at the Bass Concert Hall, complete with a giant-screen television.

To find it: 1101 Red River, Austin, Texas 78701.
Phone: 512/476-6064; for tickets, call this number or toll-free 1-888-4-MAE-STRO.
Online: www.austinsymphony.org. Tickets also may be ordered online.
Accepts: MC, Visa, Amex, Discover. Personal checks.
Hours: Mon.-Fri., 9 a.m. to 5 p.m.
Notable: Family concerts, Pops as well as classical series.

Paramount Theatre for the Performing Arts.

Designed by renowned theater architect John Eberson and built in 1915, this historic building has been carefully and lovingly restored. Now, the Paramount is as active as it was in its heyday. The theater presents all types of entertainment, from live theater to classic movies, 300 days a year.

Seating 1,300, the Paramount packs the house with everything from locally produced theater to touring productions of top musicals. Local film festivals use the Paramount to show classic and cutting-edge movies for film buffs. Austin's own Zachary Scott Theatre has produced highly successful musical revues here. Austin Musical Theatre, the resident company, has presented a string of hits, including productions for the Paramount's annual Broadway series. The Broadway series, with show dates in the fall and spring, also attracts touring companies of Broadway shows. Live musical performances, stand-up comics, and dance round out the schedule. All types of concerts—pop, jazz, ethnic, classical—have filled the Paramount with music, and both ballet and modern dance have graced the stage. These performances have included shows by Debbie Reynolds and Stomp, the percussion/dance troupe.

To find it: 713 Congress Avenue, near Seventh Street.
Phone: 512/472-5411.
Tickets: Call Star Tickets at 512/469-7469, or visit a Star Tickets outlet at Albertson's stores and other locations.
Accepts: Major credit cards for ticket purchases by telephone. Cash and checks accepted at the box office.
Notable: National Register-listed historic theater. Theater, dance, music, classic movies presented year-round.

One World. What began as an innovative arts education organization has grown to encompass its own beautiful, intimate performance space hosting performers from all over the world.

Whether it's bringing cultural arts programs and workshops to schoolchildren through Touring One World or offering performances by jazz and tango musicians, flamenco dancers and ballet through One World Theatre, One World's mission is highlighting Austin's multi-cultural heritage by bringing the arts of the world to this city. Its new, 300-seat performance venue includes state-of-the-art lighting and sound systems to help attract noteworthy performers, and its intimacy will be appreciated by performers and audiences alike.

To find it: 7701 Bee Caves Road.
Phone: 512/330-9500.
Fax: 512/330-9600.
Email: 1world@flash.net

Online: www.oneworld-online.org
Notable: Cutting-edge educational programs. World music and dance performances unlike anything else in Austin.

Apple Leasing-Star Fleet Limousine will provide transportation via Star Fleet. If you want to arrive at One World Theatre—or any special place—in style, Star Fleet is at your service with elegant automobiles and discreet drivers.

To find it: 7200 Mopac North, Suite 430.
Phone: 512/346-9977, 888/346-9977.
Mobile: 512/751-7772.
Fax: 512/346-4252.

Dallas Night Club.

Think Wednesday is just hump day? Not here. Wednesday is the hottest night of the week for Dallas Night Club, when two-steppers, jitter-buggers, and waltzers crowd the 3,000-square-foot dance floor. It's not just the country crowd that turns out, but a cross-section of Austin. Anyone and everyone can have a great time at Dallas Night Club.

Of course, dancing is the centerpiece of Dallas Night Club, and Wednesday night isn't the only night that the place is hopping. Club managers are continually amazed at the talented dancers who grace their dance floor. But beginners are just as welcome—and they'll find lots of "experts" willing to lend a hand.

If dancing isn't your favorite activity, Dallas Night Club offers a host of others. Six televisions tuned to cable are available for watching, including three of the largest big-screen TVs in town. Six pool tables provide diversion for those who like a little sport in their nights. And to quell the hunger of their customers, Dallas Night Club offers a Happy Hour buffet weekday evenings (Sundays through Friday). And you can take home a T-shirt or cap with the Dallas Night Club logo to remember your visit.

In May of 2000, Dallas Night Club will have its 20th birthday, and they're planning a huge celebration. Five weeks of parties, no less. There will be theme nights for each year the club has been open, 1980 through 1999. Plus, much more; the events are April 5th -May 5th, culminating with a huge celebration on the week of our 20th anniversary May 3rd-6th.

But you don't have to wait for a special occasion. Come to Dallas Night Club anytime and you'll be coming back for more.

To find it: 7113 Burnet Road.
Phone: 512/452-2810.
Accepts: All major credit cards and ATM cards.
Hours: Sunday to Friday 5 p.m. to 2 a.m.; Saturday 7 p.m. to 2 a.m.
Notable: Pool tables, televisions, including 3 huge big-screen TVS. 20th birthday celebration, May 2000; Happy Hour buffet Sunday to Friday, 5:30-7:30 p.m.

Speakeasy Venture down an alley in the Warehouse District to find two great, oaken doors. This is the portal to the Prohibition Era-themed live music venue, Speakeasy.

Speakeasy opened in 1997 to cater to the expanding population of high-tech professionals drawn to Austin while appealing to the locals as well. The upscale atmosphere and Prohibition theme offer something new and different to the Austin music scene.

Inside, the decor is plush and beautiful. You'll fall in love with the antique tables on the mezzanine and the clawfooted, red-felted pool table in back. Or take the elevator to the Evergreen Terrace, where you can take in a spectacular view of the downtown skyline or an awe-inspiring sunset vista to the west .

Perhaps it's the lush surroundings that inspire the clientele to put an extra polish on their attire. Get into the Speakeasy spirit. Dress up, jazz up a little. You'll feel as though you fit right in to the 1920s decor.

Check out the specialty drinks menu for some refreshing new libations, or order a classic. The bar is huge, but cozy, with comfortable stools and rows of shining liquor bottles. Or choose a table by the stage to get a close-up view of the evening's featured musicians or DJ entertainment.

Speakeasy's happy hour starts at 4p.m. weekdays. Drink specials include a dollar off mixed drinks and draft beer.

To find it: 412-D Congress Ave.
Phone: 512/476-8086.
Accepts: All major credit cards.
Hours: Monday to Friday 4 p.m. to 2 a.m.; Saturday 6 p.m. to 2 a.m. Sunday 7p.m. to 2 a.m.
Notable: Prohibition-Era decor. Live music. Happy hour weekdays.

Remember the last time you heard a Lyle Lovett song as you walked into a restaurant? Or a Stevie Ray Vaughan tune covered by a band at your favorite club? How about a ZZ Top hit on the radio?

Each time you hear music by one of these artists, they or their estates are entitled to royalties from that performance. Without royalties, songwriters, composers, lyricists and music publishers wouldn't get paid. Music enriches our lives every day—and without the American Society of Composers, Authors and Publishers, musicians would have a hard time collecting the royalties for all these many performances of their work.

Created in 1914, ASCAP is a clearinghouse for creators and users of music. ASCAP's customers, or licensees, are all those who want to perform music publicly, including symphony orchestras and shopping malls, bars and web sites. Under U.S. Copyright law, those who perform or play music must ask permission of the copyright owner and pay the appropriate fees. ASCAP gives permission to those who use music, and it collects the fees required. In turn, it pays songwriters, artists and music publishers their royalties.

ASCAP is owned and run by its members, and in Texas, Jan Mirkin of Mirkin Management (pictured above) handles ASCAP business. ASCAP represents all kinds of music, from pop and rock and country to new age and theater and symphonic music. Some of the top Texas ASCAP writers include (below, left to right) Fastball, Stevie Ray Vaughan, Lyle Lovett, ZZ Top and Ian Moore.

Mirkin Management currently manages Moore, who has toured with the Rolling Stones, Bob Dylan, and ZZ Top and currently is signed to Koch Entertainment, as well as Kitty Gordon of Matchbox Records. Founded in 1986, the company helps musicians negotiate recording and publishing contracts, establish touring schedules, market and promote themselves and their work, and plan their careers.

As ASCAP representative, Mirkin also helps songwriters, publishers and lyricists join the group. For an appointment to fill out a membership application, call 512/472-1818.

© James Innes

Scholz Garten. This old-fashioned biergarten once was a place for the entire family to come. Kids would romp around the bandstand, and their parents enjoyed good food, cold beer and live music. Well, the tradition is still alive here. In fact, Scholz hasn't changed too much since it opened in 1866. It's still a plae for students, professors and politicians to engage in political debate. It's still a spot where live music is a regular on the menu. And the beer is still cold and the food still worth the trip in itself.

To find it: 1607 San Jacinto Blvd.
Phone: 512/474-1958.
Accepts: All major credit cards, personal checks.
Hours: 11 a.m. to 11 p.m. daily.
Notable: Texas' oldest continuously operating business. Banquet facilities for up to 800. Tradition of live music, including German bands and Austin up-and-comers.

Cherry Creek Catfish Co.

Restaurant owner Shari Braly has cooked up a half-dozen awards for her barbecue, but here in South Austin it's the Southern-style menu she's winning kudos for. Headlined by its original crispy fried catfish, Cherry Creek Catfish Co. also serves up shrimp, oysters, chicken-fried steak, burgers, po-boys — not to mention Braly's award-winning ribs. Add a scrumptious selection of homemade desserts and you'll leave Cherry Creek with a sweet smile on your face.

To find it: 5712 Manchaca.
Phone: 512/440-8810.
Accepts: MC, Visa, Amex, Discover.
Hours: 11 a.m. to 9 p.m. Sundays to Thursdays; 11 a.m. to 10 p.m. Fridays and Saturdays.
Notable: Kid-friendly. Great home-baked desserts. Wide selection of menu items, fried catfish to grilled seafood.

Austin Land & Cattle Company.

They've won accolades here for their beef, hand-cut here at the restaurant. There's pork chops and chicken breast for white-meat eaters and even a portobello mushroom steak as a vegetarian option. Or try the innovative seafood: peppercorn-encrusted yellowfin tuna, South American lobster tail and more. Soups, salads and sides, not to mention dessert, are all served up by the friendly, knowledgeable staff. A full bar and an extensive wine list rounds out your meal.

To find it: 1205 N. Lamar Boulevard.
Phone: 512/472-1813.
Accepts: All major credit cards.
Hours: Sunday-Thursday 5-10 p.m.; Friday-Saturday 5-11p.m.
Notable: Award-winning aged steaks hand-cut on the premises. Fresh, innovative seafood. Voted best steak in town. Three stars from the *Austin American-Statesman*.

The Tavern.

Located in an old grocery story modeled after a German public house, this hangout has a rich history, including ghosts, politicos, soldiers and aficionados of bathtub gin. Today, it remains a meeting place, a sports bar with more than a dozen televisions and satellite sports, a student hangout. Ice-cold beer and home-cooked meals keep 'em coming back, and don't miss all those stories carved into the bar. As they say around here, you're never too far from 12th and Lamar.

To find it: 12th St. and Lamar Blvd.
Phone: 512/474-7496.
Accepts: Major credit cards.
Hours: 11 a.m. to 2 a.m. daily.
Notable: Happy Hour weekdays 3-7 p.m. Daily Lunch specials. Coldest beer in Austin. Sports bar with 13 televisions and satellite programming. Resident ghost likes the sound of breaking glass.

Pacifica. Step into this restaurant and find yourself in the tropics. The atmosphere evokes a British Colonial plantation on a South Sea island, and the glittering cuisine presented on crisp white table linens brings that region's flavor to life. Fresh seafood is featured, but beef, pork, chicken and vegetarian dishes round out the menu. Presented with panache, everything from appetizer to dessert reflects the vibrant tastes of the Pacific, the most sophisticated culinary landscape in the world. Desserts vary daily.

To find it: 3801 Capital of Texas Highway, Suite A180. In Davenport Village.
Phone: 512/327-3332.
Fax: 512/327-5528.
Accepts: MC, Visa, Amex, Diners, Discover.
Hours: 11:30 a.m. to 2 p.m. Monday-Friday; 5:30-10 p.m. Monday-Thursday; 5:30-11pm Friday-Saturday; 10:30 a.m. to 2 p.m. Sunday.

County Line Restaurants. Both County Line locations serve excellent barbecue —from ribs to brisket to chicken and more — in a Texas roadhouse atmosphere.
County Line on the Hill. Perched on one of the highest hills in the area, this County Line offers a 20-mile view of the Texas Hill country to enjoy with steak, fish and kabobs.

To find it: 6500 W. Bee Caves Road.
Phone: 512/327-1742.
Accepts: All major credit cards.
Hours: Dinner only, seven days a week.

County Line on the Lake. Set in an old lake lodge. Specialties include smoked prime rib and smoked pork tenderloin. Accessible by boat.

To find it: 5204 F.M. 2222.
Phone: 512/346-3664.
Accepts: All major credit cards.
Hours: Lunch and dinner, seven days.

Green Mesquite BBQ & More. The barbeque and the atmosphere here has a 50-year-old-plus pedigree. It still carries out a tradition of live music on the patio, inviting many of those we now watch on Austin City Limits to play. The brisket still smokes 16 hours or more. The same patio still serves as a stage for great live music on weekends, including traditional bluegrass on Sundays. Pecan trees still arch overhead and you can still count fireflies at no extra charge while you enjoy your barbeque or burger.

To find it: 1400 Barton Springs Road. In North Austin at Hwy 183 and Anderson Mill Road. In Oak Hill at Hwys 71 and 290.
Phone: 512/479-0485.
Accepts: Major credit cards, personal checks.
Hours: 11 a.m. to 11 p.m. daily.
Notable: Long-smoked brisket. Live music on the patio. Annual fiddle contest each fall.

El Arroyo. This local chain of casual Tex-Mex restaurants has been serving up Austin's favorite foods for more than a decade in an atmosphere dubbed "early tacky". Now with three locations and catering service, El Arroyo is never far away when you get a hankering for your favorite tacos, enchiladas and other Mexican specialties. Try the spinach enchiladas or Del Mar enchiladas stuffed with crab and shrimp. And take home a T-shirt or baseball cap to remember your visit.

To find it: 1624 W. Fifth, Austin; 301 E. Hwy. 79, Round Rock; 7032 Wood Hollow Drive.
Phone: 512/474-1222 (5th St.), 345-TACO (Far West), 310-1992 (Round Rock).
Accepts: Major credit cards.
Hours: Mon.-Tue. 11 a.m. to 10 p.m.; Wed.-Thu. 11 a.m. to 11 p.m.; Fri., 11 a.m. to midnight; Sat. 10 a.m. to midnight; Sun. 10 a.m. to 10 p.m.

Castle Hill Cafe. Always ranked among Austin's best, this comfortable restaurant offers affordable dining in a warm, eclectic setting. The feeling is casual, and the original art and ceramics and Oaxacan animal carvings invite the eye to linger. But what really makes dining at Castle Hill a treat is the wonderful, creative food. Classified as "New Continental," the menu includes such favorites as lamb empanadas, pad Thai, duck and sausage gumbo, and a mocha toffee torte. Whether for a party or a quiet dinner for two, Castle Hill is the perfect venue for a stellar meal.

To find it: 1101 W. Fifth Street.
Phone: 512/486-0728.
Accepts: Visa, MC, Amex, Discover.
Hours: Lunch served 11 a.m. to 2:30 p.m. Mon.-Fri. Dinner 6-10 p.m. Mon.-Sat. Closes between Christmas and New Year's and the week of July 4.
Notable: Consistently among Austin's favorite fine dining destinations. Private dining rooms available for parties Mondays-Thursdays for up to 47.

Jeffrey's. If Austin has a culinary landmark, this is it. Jeffrey's was Austin's first upscale dining spot, and many say it's still the best. Executive Chef David Garrido's pitch-perfect palate has yielded a culinary style exclusively his: a masterful blend of Southwest and Latin tastes with continental technique. The result is vivid, sophisticated food that lingers in the memory and pairs beautifully with wine. Add the restaurant's warm, friendly service and a *Wine Spectator*-lauded wine list, and you have the most well-rounded dining experience in the city. No wonder Austinites select it as their favorite year after year.

To find it: 1204 W. Lynn Street.
Phone: 512/477-5584.
Accepts: Major credit cards.
Hours: Monday-Thursday from 6 p.m. Friday-Sunday from 5:30 p.m.

Mirabelle. The interplay of food and wine takes center stage at this neighborhood restaurant, which has taken Austin by storm. The contemporary American cuisine is spiced with various world flavors, including French, Italian, Asian and Southwestern. Among the taste-tempting dishes are the picadillo empenadas, the blackened Gulf shrimp with Gorgonzola cream and the Mushroom-crusted lamb with Balsamic jus. Or come for brunch and try the Eggs Benedict with citrus hollandaise. The Mediterranean-style decor showcases the work of local artists.

To find it: 8127 Mesa Drive.
Phone: 512/346-7900.
Accepts: Visa, MC, Amex, Diners.
Hours: Lunch served 11 a.m. to 2 p.m. Mon.-Fri. Dinner 5:30-9:30 p.m. Mon.-Thurs., 5:30-10 p.m. Fri.-Sat. Sunday Brunch 10:30 a.m. to 2 p.m.

Shoreline Grill. The team behind Austin's dining superstar, Jeffrey's, brings sophisticated, eclectic dining to downtown Austin with this eatery overlooking Town Lake. From business power lunches to distinctive dinners, Shoreline Grill offers meals that reflect their origins in fresh, quality ingredients, in an atmosphere of comfortable elegance. It doesn't hurt that the dining room and balcony offer stunning views of the lake and the restaurant's famous neighbor, the Congress Avenue Bat Colony, which wheels into the sky in the summer sunset.

To find it: 98 San Jacinto Blvd.
Phone: 512/477-3300 for reservations; 477-7598 for private events.
Fax: 512/477-6392.
Accepts: Major credit cards.
Hours: Lunch Mondays-Fridays from 11:00 a.m.; dinner nightly from 5:00 p.m.

The Driskill Hotel. This grande dame of Austin recently got a face lift—and what a face lift it is. The Driskill truly is a grand hotel in the old style, once again. The Driskill originally opened in 1886, and today, following a three-year, $35 million restoration, it has returned to its original, luxurious Victorian splendor.

With one step into the stunning lobby, you'll find yourself surrounded by beautiful craftsmanship, luxurious materials and authentic Victorian furnishings. An intricate hand-laid marble floor ushers guests inside. A painstakingly hand-painted decorative ceiling draws the eye upwards to a majestic, stained glass dome custom-made for The Driskill. Its radiant beauty even eclipses the fine period furnishings and original artwork, and it illustrates the attention to detail one finds throughout this fine hotel.

Each of the hotel's 205 rooms and suites has been completely remade and outfitted in turn-of-the-century Victorian style. Custom-made wrought-iron beds, Texas-sized original furnishings, original artwork and rich fabrics create a feeling of old world elegance. Bathrooms are richly appointed with either black Brazilian marble or black-and-white tile, each true to the Victorian period. And while the surroundings seem to sweep one back in time, the appointments offer all the convenience of the present, from in-room high-speed T1 connections to dual-line telephones and personal safes, to mention a few.

This convenience and opulence is paired, like fine wine and food, with the hospitality of a well-trained and thoughtful staff. The Driskill turns hospitality into an art form. Endowed with experience, attention and discretion, the staff works constantly to make each guest's visit a flawless experience beyond their grandest expectations.

Their expertise extends to the renowned Driskill Grill & Bar, a haven for those who want to relax over a 20-year-old whisky or sample a sumptuous meal. In comfortable, elegant surroundings, diners can feast on the inventive cuisine of Executive Chef David J. Bull, a classically trained chef grounded in his Italian family's love for food. Whether a breakfast of eggs and chorizo hash, a luncheon of a grilled tuna steak sandwich or penne chicken pasta, or a dinner of lobster and sirloin, or crisp Chilean Sea Bass pan broiled with Saffron and Dill served over wild mushrooms, artichokes and asperagus.

The Driskill's expert hospitality and opulent surroundings are the perfect backdrop for business meetings and special events as well. The staff delights in hosting one-of-a-kind gatherings, whether intimate dinners in one of the charming private rooms or grand occasions in the majestic ballroom.

To find it: 604 Brazos Street.
Phone: 512/474-5911, 800/252-9367.
Fax: 512/474-2214.
Accepts: All major credit cards.
Hours: 24 hours daily. Check in, 3 p.m. Check out, noon. **The Driskill Grill:** Serving breakfast, lunch, dinner and Sunday brunch. 6:30 a.m. -2 p.m. and 5:30-10 p.m. daily. **Bar:** 11 a.m. to midnight Sunday-Thursday; 11 a.m. to 2 a.m. Friday-Saturday.
Notable: Recently completed $35 million, complete historic restoration. A member of The Leading Hotels of the World, and National Trust Historic Hotels of America. Adjacent to Sixth Street, just blocks from the Texas Capitol and Town Lake.

Vintage Villas. Whether you're looking for a spectacular getaway spot or a venue for a corporate retreat, this lovely hotel on Lake Travis will fit your needs.

It's just a short drive from Austin to Vintage Villas, but the setting takes you far from the hustle and bustle of urban life. Here you can focus exclusively on your corporate meeting—or on your special companion.

Vintage Villas is actually three villas, each with its own atmosphere and comforts reflecting the heritage of three Texas regions: South, Central and East. Each of the 43 rooms overlooks the lake and is well-equipped to help you relax. Most of them have balconies so you can enjoy the view in the open air. Furnished with antiques and handmade furniture selected to carry out the regional theme, the rooms also have high-tech amenities such as a 27-inch television with built-in VCR, microwave and refrigerator with ice-maker, and access for phone, computer and fax. A built-in bar sink and coffeemaker put your favorite refreshments close at hand, and a complimentary breakfast is served bed-and-breakfast style

every morning. Suites and Jacuzzi tubs are available by request.

The facilities also include meeting and event rooms to accommodate up to 200 people. Audiovisual equipment is available. Full-kitchen catering is offered for lunch, dinner, snacks and breaks.

Golfers will appreciate the easy access to three excellent championship golf courses. Nearby marinas are your entree to fun on the lake, including watercraft rentals. Wine lovers will appreciate the short walk to the tasting rooms and tour at the Slaughter/Leftwich winery.

To find it: 4209 Eck Lane.
Phone: 512/266-9333.
Accepts: MC, Visa, Amex, Discover, Diners. Personal checks with proper ID.
Hours: 6:30 a.m.-10:30 p.m. daily.
Notable: Beautiful view of Lake Travis. Spa, gym. Complimentary breakfast and beverages. Mini-kitchen in each room.

Downtown in Full Moon
By Linda Dumont

In a city full of Tex-Mex haunts, it's no surprise that huevos rancheros and migas show up on so many menus here. Maybe that's why brunch is such a hallowed Austin tradition. Truly, you haven't experienced Austin until you've parked on a restaurant patio and lingered over a breakfast taco, while drinking coffee and reading the newspaper. But don't despair if you've had enough of that ubiquitous specimen—just sample a different kind of cuisine for brunch or lunch. Vietnamese? New continental? Vegetarian? This city has them all.

Brownings. A family-owned restaurant, Brownings offers fresh, homemade sandwiches, quiches, casseroles, as well as beautiful desserts, all served in a homey, cozy dining room. Don't miss the fresh-baked bread or out-of-this world desserts.

To find it: No. 4 Salado Square, Main Street, Salado, Texas.
Phone: 254/947-8666.
Fax: 254/947-8675.
Accepts: MC, Visa. Personal checks with ID.
Hours: Daily 11 a.m. to 4 p.m.

The Stagecoach Inn. In years past, this Chisholm Trail stop welcomed Gen. George Custer and the notorious James brothers. Today, the lovely landmark's frontier heritage is preserved in a down-home atmosphere where you'll find the best in country food. The Inn's two eateries offer Texas menus built around original farm and ranch recipes. Traditional favorites such as plate-size steaks and fried chicken join unique appetizers and desserts like tomato aspic and banana fritters — plus the tastiest hush puppies in Texas.

To find it: Interstate 35, take exit 283 or 284.
Phone: 800/732-8994.
Accepts: MC, Visa, Amex, Discover. Personal checks.
Hours: Seven days a week, 11 a.m. to 4 p.m. and 5-9 p.m.

Rose Cottage Gifts and Antiques, Pink Rose Tearoom. The four McLaurin sisters can cook with a real Southern style. Every day, they prepare a chef's special and a soup of the day. The regular menu includes the Pink Rose's famous sandwiches, made with fresh, home-baked bread, and entrees such as chicken spaghetti, pasta salad, and baked potatoes. Delectable desserts are made daily.

To find it: 102 North Main.
Phone: 254/947-9110.
Accepts: Visa, Amex, Discover, and personal checks, with identification.
Hours: 11 a.m. to 3 p.m. weekdays, 11 a.m. to 5 p.m. weekends. Closed Tues.

Pacifica. This restaurant evokes a British Colonial plantation on a South Sea island, and the glittering cuisine brings that region's flavor to life. Presented with panache, everything from appetizer to dessert reflects the vibrant tastes of the Pacific, the most sophisticated culinary landscape in the world. Desserts vary daily.

To find it: 3801 Capital of Texas Highway, Suite A180. Austin, Texas 78746.
Phone: 512/327-3332.
Fax: 512/327-5528.
Accepts: All major credit cards.
Hours: 11:30 a.m. to 2 p.m. Monday-Friday; 5:30-10 p.m. Monday-Thursday; 5:30-11pm Friday-Saturday; 10:30 a.m. to 2 p.m. Sunday.

Thistle Cafe. The heavenly smells that greet customers at this American-style bistro are reason enough to stop by. We guarantee you'll stay for a taste. The Thistle serves high-quality food fashioned from fresh ingredients in an atmosphere that is casual and fun, yet elegant. Make sure to sample some of the delectable cookies and other desserts! And try the migas for Sunday brunch. Take-out meals are available seven days.

To find it: 3801 Capital of Texas Highway, Suite C200.
Phone: 512/347-1000.
Accepts: MC, Visa, Amex, Diners.
Hours: 9 a.m. to 9 p.m. Monday through Thursday. 9 a.m. to 9:30 p.m. Friday. 8 a.m. to 9:30 p.m. Saturday. 8 a.m. to 3 p.m. Sunday.

Trudy's. A local favorite for more than 20 years, Trudy's serves up award-winning margaritas and Hondo-sized portions of the best Tex-Mex and Southern-style cuisine. Check out their website for menus, directions and hours.

To find it: Three locations: South Austin at 4141 Capital of Texas Hwy. South. Central at 409 W. 30th St. North at 8820 Burnet Road.
Phone: 512/ 326-9899 (south), 477-2935 (central) and 454-1474 (north).
Online: www.trudys.com
Accepts: Major credit cards.

The Filling Station.

They're famous for their huge, three-quarter-pound hamburgers, but this restaurant offers an eclectic menu of crisp salads, tender chicken-fried steak, and sizzling fajitas. All of the food is prepared in-house, daily—always fresh, never frozen. Whatever you order, you'll feel comfortable in this casual, fun atmosphere of old car and gas-station memorabilia. Finish off your meal with one of the delicious dessert selections. Reservations accepted, but unnecessary.

To find it: 801 Barton Springs Road.
Phone: 512/477-1022.
Email: fsaustin@aol.com
Accepts: Visa, MC, Discover, Amex, Diners.
Hours: Monday-Thursday 11 a.m. to midnight; Friday-Saturday 11 a.m. to 2 a.m.; Sunday noon to midnight.

Green Mesquite BBQ & More.

The barbeque and the atmosphere here has a 50-year-old-plus pedigree. The brisket still smokes 16 hours or more. The same patio still serves as a stage for great live music on weekends, including traditional bluegrass on Sundays. You can still count fireflies at no extra charge while you enjoy your barbeque or burger.

To find it: 1400 Barton Springs Road. In North Austin at Hwy 183 and Anderson Mill Road. In Oak Hill at Hwys 71 and 290.
Phone: 512/479-0485.
Accepts: Major credit cards, personal checks.
Hours: 11 a.m. to 11 p.m. daily.

Cherry Creek Catfish Co.

Restaurant owner Shari Braly has cooked up a half-dozen awards for her barbecue, but here in South Austin it's the Southern-style menu she's winning kudos for. Headlined by its original crispy fried catfish, Cherry Creek Catfish Co. also serves up shrimp, oysters, chicken-fried steak, burgers, po-boys — not to mention Braly's award-winning ribs and desserts.

To find it: 5712 Manchaca.
Phone: 512/440-8810.
Accepts: MC, Visa, Amex, Discover.
Hours: 11 a.m. to 9 p.m. Sundays to Thursdays; 11 a.m. to 10 p.m. Fridays and Saturdays.

El Sol y La Luna. This cozy, casual, art-lined café if your ticket to award-winning Mexican specialties. El Sol y La Luna is consistently chosen as one of Austin's favorite restaurants. Breakfast is served all day, whether migas or huevos motuleños or the best pozole in town. If you're hankering for a crispy taco or enchilada, you've come to the right place as well. The enchiladas rojas are award-winners. Or try one of El Sol y La Luna's many specialties, including some of the finest interior Mexican food around.

To find it: 1224 S. Congress Ave.
Phone: 512/444-7770.
Accepts: All major credit cards.
Hours: Sun.-Tues. 7 a.m. to 3 p.m.; Wed.-Sat. 7 a.m. to 10 p.m.

Coffee Fever 2
By Linda Dumont

El Arroyo. This local chain of casual Tex-Mex restaurants serves up Austin's favorite foods in an atmosphere dubbed "early tacky". Now with three locations, El Arroyo is never far away when you get a hankering for your favorite tacos, enchiladas and other Mexican specialties.
To find it: 1624 W. Fifth, Austin; 301 E. Hwy. 79, Round Rock; 7032 Wood Hollow Drive, Austin.
Phone: 512/474-1222 (5th St.), 345-TACO (Far West), 310-1992 (Round Rock).
Accepts: Major credit cards.
Hours: Mon.-Tue. 11 a.m. to 10 p.m.; Wed.-Thu. 11 a.m. to 11 p.m.; Fri. 11 a.m. to midnight; Sat. 10 a.m. to midnight; Sun. 10 a.m. to 10 p.m.

Triumph Cafe & Gift Shop.
Soon after Truc Nguyen started this coffee-and-pastry shop, his customers persuaded him to add Vietnamese food to the menu. Now, it's possible to visit Triumph for a breakfast bagel or croissant, a luncheon sandwich served on homemade European flatbread, and a Vietnamese dinner of spring rolls, vermicelli, noodle soup, and steamed rice dishes. And a specialty espresso drink, hot tea or chai along with dessert.
To find it: 3808 Spicewood Springs Rd.
Phone: 512/343-1875.
Accepts: Major credit cards, checks.
Hours: 7 a.m. to 9 p.m. Monday-Thursday; 7 a.m. to 11 p.m. Friday; 8 a.m. to 11 p.m. Saturday; 9 a.m. to 3 p.m. Sunday.

Mirabelle.
The interplay of food and wine takes center stage at this neighborhood restaurant, which has taken Austin by storm. The contemporary American cuisine is spiced with various world flavors, including French, Italian, Asian and Southwestern. Among the taste-tempting dishes are the picadillo empenadas, the blackened Gulf shrimp with Gorgonzola cream and the Eggs Benedict with citrus hollandaise.
To find it: 8127 Mesa Drive.
Phone: 512/346-7900.
Accepts: Visa, MC, Amex, Diners.
Hours: 11 a.m. to 2 p.m. Mon.-Fri. 5:30-9:30 p.m. Mon.-Thurs., 5:30-10 p.m. Fri.-Sat. Sunday Brunch 10:30 a.m. to 2 p.m.

Central Market.
Don't feel like cooking? Stop by Central Market's Cafe on the Run, where you'll find chef-prepared salads and sandwiches, as well as main-and side-dish fare to take home. Or relax at the Central Market Cafe, which showcases the best of the store's fresh ingredients.
To find it: 4001 N. Lamar Blvd. in Central Park; 4477 S. Lamar Blvd. at Ben White.
Phone: 512/206-1000 north, 899-4300 south.
Accepts: Major cards. Personal checks.
Hours: Central: 7 a.m. to 10 p.m. daily.
South: Sunday-Thursday 7 a.m. to 10 p.m.; Friday-Saturday 7 a.m. to 11 p.m.

Chez Zee.
This casually elegant cafe and bakery is great for a business lunch or a special meal—or stop by anytime for one of their luscious signature desserts. House specialties include Mediterranean Pasta, Tequila Lime Chicken Grille and a Pecan-Crusted Chicken Caesar. Breakfast and and brunch dishes are also standouts; try the French Toast made from challah and creme brulee. Local artists show their work on the walls among the owners' excellent private collection.
To find it: 5406 Balcones.
Phone: 512/454-2666.
Accepts: Major credit cards.
Hours: M-Thurs 11 a.m.-10:30 p.m.
Fri-Sat. 9 a.m.-Midnight
Sun. 9-3 Brunch 3-10 p.m. grille/dinner.

The Tavern. This hangout has a rich history, including ghosts, politicos, soldiers and aficionados of bathtub gin. Today, it remains a meeting place, a sports bar with more than a dozen televisions and satellite sports, a student hangout. Ice-cold beer and home-cooked meals keep 'em coming back, and don't miss all those stories carved into the bar.

To find it: 12th St. and Lamar Blvd.
Phone: 512/474-7496.
Accepts: Major credit cards.
Hours: 11 a.m. to 2 a.m. daily.

Apple Annie's They opened their doors in 1982 aiming to provide healthy gourmet food to Austin. At Apple Annie's Café Express downtown, you can have breakfast or lunch on weekdays, either inside or outdoors in the open-air courtyard. Feast on homemade salads or sandwiches made on their bakery bread. Hot entrees range from pastas and pizza to grilled chicken, fish and meatloaf. The menu changes daily. And don't forget to sample Apple Annie's baked goods.

To find it: 221 W. Sixth St. in Bank One Tower.
Phone: 512/472-1884.
Accepts: MC, Visa, Amex. Personal checks with proper ID.
Hours: Cafe and Bakery: Monday to Friday 7 a.m. to 2 p.m.

The Driskill Grill & Bar. A haven for those who want to relax over a 20-year-old whisky or sample a sumptuous meal. In comfortable, elegant surroundings, diners can feast on the inventive cuisine of Chef David Bull. Whether a breakfast of eggs and chorizo hash, a luncheon of a grilled tuna steak sandwich or penne chicken pasta, or a dinner of lobster and sirloin, Bull's menu delivers traditional favorites with an unexpected twist of tastes.

To find it: 604 Brazos Street.
Phone: 512/474-5911, 800/252-9367.
Accepts: All major credit cards.
Hours: 6 a.m. -2 p.m. and 5:30-10 p.m. daily. **Bar:** 11 a.m. to midnight Sun.-Thurs.; 1 a.m. to 2 a.m. Fri.-Sat.

Scholz Garten. This old-fashioned biergarten once was a place for the entire family. Kids would romp around the bandstand, and their parents enjoyed good food, cold beer and live music. Well, the tradition is still alive here. It's still a place for students, professors and politicians to engage in political debate. It's still a spot where live music is a regular on the menu. And the beer is still cold and the food still worth the trip in itself.

To find it: 1607 San Jacinto Blvd.
Phone: 512/474-1958.
Accepts: All major credit cards, personal checks.
Hours: 11 a.m. to 11 p.m. daily.

Fresh Planet Cafe. Located inside the flagship Whole Foods Market, this restaurant serves up fresh cuisine in a warm, casual atmosphere. Bright colors and dark wood accents create a friendly place for a quick snack or pleasurable meal. Designed by the executive chef of Jeffrey's, David Garrido, the menu offers up Asian and Mexican specialties built with fresh ingredients. Sandwiches, salads, entrees, wraps and smoothies all are available via counter service for eat-in or take-out.

To find it: 601 N. Lamar, Suite 200.
Phone: 512/476-0902.
Accepts: All major credit cards, personal checks.
Hours: Mon.-Sat. 11 a.m. to 9 p.m.; Sun. 9 a.m. to 4 p.m.

Coffee Fever 1
By Linda Dumont

Georgetown

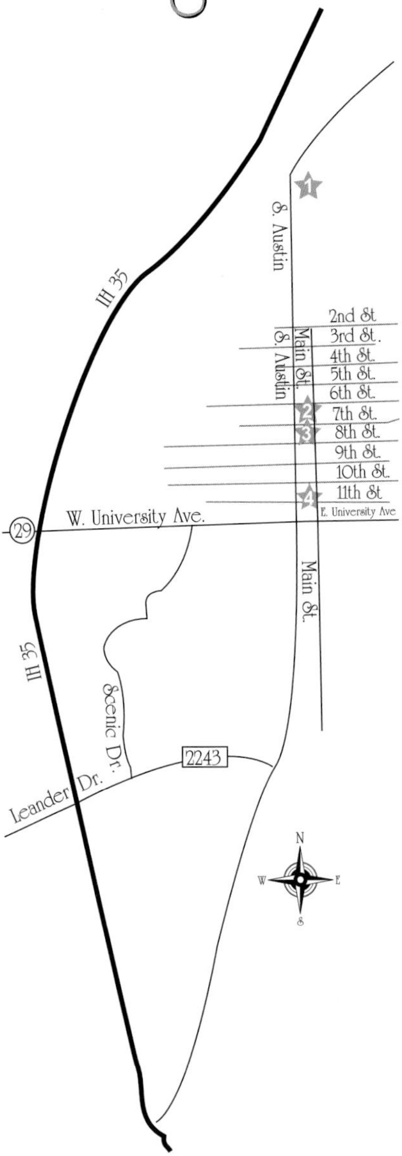

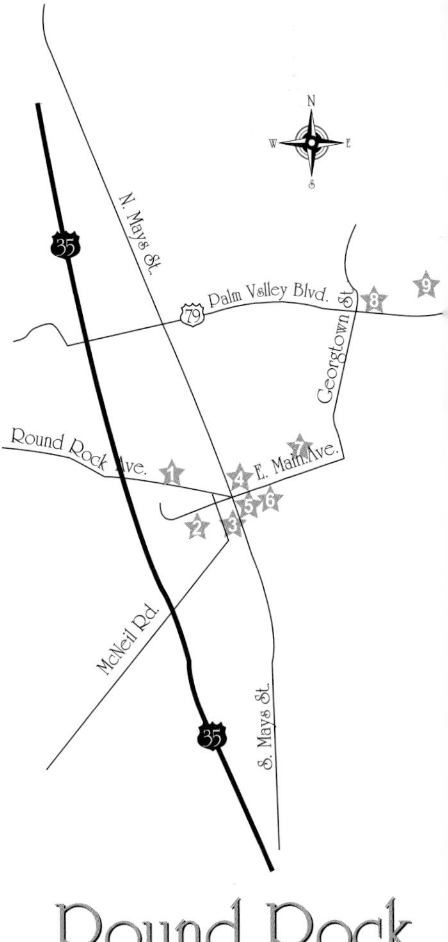

IH 35

S. Austin

🌟 1

2nd St.
3rd St.
4th St.
5th St.
6th St.
7th St.
8th St.
9th St.
10th St.
11th St.

Main St.
S. Austin

🌟 2
🌟 3

29 W. University Ave.
E. University Ave

🌟 4

IH 35

Scenic Dr.

Main St.

Leander Dr.
2243

N
W   E
S

Round Rock

35

N. Mays St.

N
W   E
S

Palm Valley Blvd.
79

Georgetown St.

🌟 8
🌟 9

Round Rock Ave.
🌟 1

E. Main Ave.
🌟 4
🌟 5 🌟 6

🌟 2
🌟 3 🌟 7

McNeil Rd.

35

S. Mays St.

Set as it is on the edge of the Texas Hill Country, Austin is the perfect home base for day-trippers. The small towns on Austin's fringe have scenery, shopping, dining, and history to spare. Seeking a picturesque place to spend some time? Try the lovely village of Salado and its spectacular shopping and beautiful old homes. Or the art galleries and gift shops of Wimberly and Dripping Springs. For something different, drive southwest and take in Barsana Dham, the Southwest's largest Hindu temple.

9 **Round Rock Express**
The AA Texas League affiliate of the Houston Astros.

The Round Rock Express is owned and operated by Round Rock Baseball, Inc. Among the shareholders of this corporation are baseball legend, Nolan Ryan and his Son Reid. Baseball fans in the area honored Nolan with the adoption of the "Express" name.

Located just north of Austin, in the heart of Central Texas, Round Rock continues to grow exponentially each year. Thousands of families, who are on the high tech fast track, move to the area for a better quality of life. The Express wants to share the excitement and affordability of Minor League Baseball with its new neighbors.

The stadium is located on Highway 79, about 3.5 miles east of IH-35. The Express anticipates an opening attendance in excess of 450,000 fans. The new state-of-the-art ballpark will have 7,816 fixed seats with cupholders, 24 luxury suites and a grassy berm in the outfield with seating for an additional 2,500 fans. In addition to the stadium, the Express will have a pool and a kids play area with clears visibility of the field.

There will also be a Conference Center with a capacity of 500-650 people. This will be wired to convention center standards as to accommodate trade, craft and car shows. This facility will be available year around for use by community organizations, companies and individuals.

In January, Dell Computer announced that it has teamed with the Express. When the first ball is thrown, it will do so in the Dell Diamond stadium. Dell officials announced that they will start an "All Star" academic incentive programs at schools .

The 2000 season begins April 6, and the home opener is April 16. Call 512-255-2255 for additional information.
To find it: Highway 79, about 3.5 miles east of IH-35.
Phone: 512/255-2255.

1 **The Railyard:** The official store and ticket office for the Round Rock Express, the class AA affiliate of the Houston Astros, The Railyard is the exclusive retailer of Nolan Ryan merchandise, official hats and jerseys. In addition to men's sportswear, the store sells ladies' merchandise, including straw hats, polo shirts and accessories. Youth and infant merchandise is available as well.
To find it: 34 Round Rock Avenue. Will be moving to Stadium in April.
Phone: 512/244-1831.
Accepts: Visa, MC, Discover, AMEX.
Hours: Mon.-Fri. 10 a.m. to 6 p.m. Sat. 10 a.m. to 4 p.m.

8 **El Arroyo.** This local chain of casual Tex-Mex restaurants serves up Austin's favorite foods in an atmosphere dubbed "early tacky". Now with three locations, El Arroyo is never far away when you get a hankering for your favorite tacos, enchiladas and other Mexican specialties.
To find it: 1624 W. Fifth, Austin; 301 E. Hwy. 79, Round Rock; 7032 Wood Hollow Drive, Austin.
Phone: 512/474-1222 (5th St.), 345-TACO (Far West), 310-1992 (Round Rock).
Accepts: Major credit cards.
Hours: Mon.-Tue., 11 a.m. to 10 p.m.; Wed.-Thu., 11 a.m. to 11 p.m.; Fri., 11 a.m. to midnight; Sat. 10 a.m. to midnight; Sun. 10 a.m. to 10 p.m.

5 **Saradora's Coffeehouse:** The oldest building in old historic downtown Round Rock, Saradora's provides the community with a full espresso bar and cafe, and an ambience which invites you to spend time alone, playing games or just chatting with friends. The walls are lined with original paintings and photographs by local talent, and live music is played nightly. Sample the homemade fudge. The gifts are unique and the gift baskets, delightful. They can help plan and cater any special occasion..

To find it: 101 W. Main. East on Hwy 620 at Interstate 35.
Phone: 512/310-1200.
Email: saradora@mindspring.com
Accepts: Visa, MC, Amex, Discover.
Hours: Mon.-Thurs. 6 a.m. to 10 p.m.; Fri.-Sat. 6 a.m. to midnight; Sun. 7 a.m. to 10 p.m.

3 **Island Texas** offers brightly colored Hawaiian-style shirts, shorts, skirts, vests, aprons, dresses and western shirts crafted from prints with tropical fish, birds, florals, geckos and lizards, or tropical scenes. Perfect for any occasion when daring to be different is the rule: vacations, family reunions, golf tournaments, or a mid-life crisis change of wardrobe.

To find it: 105 S. Mays, Round Rock.
Phone: 512/218-4668.
Accepts: Visa, MC, Discover, AMEX.
Hours: Tues.-Sat. 10 a.m. to 7 p.m.

4 **Itty Bitty World:** One of the most outstanding, unique and interesting miniature dollhouse stores in Central Texas. A complete, full-line Miniature shop specializing in dollhouses, miniatures, accessories and building supplies—everything you need to build, finish and furnish your dollhouse. Something for the beginner, and everything for the advanced, enthusiastic collector.

To find it: 102 E. Main Street.
Phone: 512/310-1188.

Accepts: Visa, MC, Discover, AMEX.
Hours: Tues.-Sat. 10 a.m. to 6 p.m.

6 **Main Street Grill:** Located in the heart of historic downtown, Main Street Grill is an upscale restaurant with indoor and outdoor seating. Some of the outstanding cuisine includes Asian seared venison medallions, slow-roasted prime rib, shrimp scampi, jumbo lump crab cakes, and Arizona egg rolls. Full-service bar with an extensive wine list.

To find it: 118 E Main St.
Phone: 244-7525.
Accepts: Visa, MC, Discover, AMEX.
Hours: Breakfast Mon.-Fri. 7-9 a.m.; Lunch Mon.-Fri. 11 a.m. to 2 p.m.; Dinner Mon.-Thu. 5-10 p.m. and Fri.-Sat. 5-11 p.m.

2 **Main Street 101** offers a unique blend of women's apparel, sterling silver jewelry, and exotic home furnishings. If you are looking for "something different" for your home, this is your answer. All items are well-crafted with a style all their own. Whether a new lamp for the den, a new ring for your finger, or an outfit for that special weekend, you will not find a shop in Central Texas that offers the same style and uniqueness.

To find it: 101 W. Main Street.
Phone: 512/248-9200
Accepts: Visa, MC, Discover, AMEX.
Hours: Tues.-Sat. 10 a.m. to 6 p.m.

7 **Paper Dragon, Etc.** A unique and unusual gift and stationery shop offering a full selection of the Boyd's Bears Collection, Village Candles, Mary Engelbreit, Camille Beckman products and an array of carefully selected items. Truly a shop for all seasons where you are welcome to browse.

To find it: 112 E. Main Street
Phone: 512/255-2227
Accepts: Visa, MC, Discover.
Hours: Mon.-Sat. 10 a.m. to 5:30 p.m.

Salado

35

Salado Plaza Dr.

Stagecoach Rd.

Main St.

Van Bibber

Van Bibber

Van Bibber

35

2268

N
W   E
S

Dripping
Springs

To Austin

Hsy 290

Hwy 290

Kit Carson Dr.

Daniel Boone Rd.

Hwy 290

To Dripping
Springs

N
W   E
S

Nuttly Brown Rd.

Signal Hill Rd.

4 **Wonderful Things.**
Sharon McCarty has been a fixture in Georgetown retail for 15 years, and for good reason. She knows what women like.

Her latest venture, a cozy gift boutique called Wonderful Things, provides ample evidence of her finesse in selecting just the right merchandise. Designed to be the destination of choice for gift-buyers, the shop provides a wide selection

of, well, Wonderful Things, to give to loved ones — or to oneself.

The boutique is four rooms, each with a specific theme. The bed and bath room is an oasis of pampering products. Try Aromatique aromatherapy bath products and candles. Tub tea in formulations for stress relief and sore muscles, for example. One hundred percent cotton terrycloth robes. Glycerin soap by the slice. And much more.

The garden room provides a relaxing atmosphere for shopping, with the tinkle of a fountain and the music of windchimes. Items especially for the gardener include journals, soap, seed greeting cards, personalized garden markers, etc.

Find special baby gifts and gourmet food items in the next room. New and unusual items are

added to the children's collection often, and the food products — sauces, marinades, spreads and more — come with friendly advice on how and when to use them.

The fourth room is devoted to the Brighton brand, and because Wonderful Things is a "Heart" store for Brighton, the selection is large and varied. The traditional Brighton belts, handbags and other small leather goods of course are on display, but also new and different lines, such as hair accessories, jewelry and even four signature fragrances. If this variety doesn't persuade you that Wonderful Things is committed to Brighton, look for the "Brighton Bug" (pictured above) parked out front.

The attentive staff makes gift shopping easy with their friendly service and knowledgable suggestions. In fact, busy folks can call Wonderful Things, provide a few guidelines, and the staff will assemble a gorgeous gift basket for pickup or delivery. But I recommend shopping in person. It's a pleasure one shouldn't miss.

To find it: 1100 South Main Street (near the intersection of Main and University) Georgetown, Texas 78626.
Phone: 512/863-3411.
Accepts: MC, Visa, Amex, Discover, and personal checks.
Hours: 9:30-5:00 Monday-Saturday, closed Sunday and holidays. **Shipping:** Available through UPS, $5.75/package.
Notable: Gift wrap free with $10 purchase. Phone-in gift basket service available. Mailing-list customers receive birthday coupons.

3 Hill Country Bookstore.

The comfortable, over-stuffed chairs at the end of each set of bookshelves are the first hint of welcome here. The friendly smiles and helpful service cinch it -- Hill Country Bookstore is a perfect place to find a great book, relax and maybe meet some new friends.

This family-owned and -operated bookstore is in the cornerstone building on the historical downtown Georgetown square. This lovely old building lends its ambiance to the shelves filled with books on Texas and American history.

The environment here is relaxing and comfortable. To avid readers, it's mesmerizing. Whatever your interest, you'll find a volume on it here. Wander through the stacks, and you will discover bestsellers, science fiction, gardening books, self-help tomes, and inspirational and religious works.

The bookshelves also reveal Owner Margarite Holt's commitment to local talent. Many books by local authors are showcased here. Holt also has invited local artists and members of the Williamson County Art Guild to show their work. These displays give Hill Country Bookstore a flavor all its own.

Margarite's goal of providing a "unique environment where books and people meet" is definitely realized at Hill Country Bookstore. Stop by and read a while.

To find it: 719 S. Main St., Georgetown, Texas 78626.
Phone: 512/869-4959.
Fax: 512/869-5525.
Accepts: MC, Visa, Amex, and personal checks.
Hours: 10:00-6:00 Monday-Saturday, 1:00-5:00 Sunday.
Notable: Local authors and artists' work available.

2 Georgetown Antique Mall.

The hallmark of Georgetown Antique Mall is quality. Not only is all the merchandise highly collectible, the shop also offers a variety of services so that customers know exactly what they're getting.

First, there's access to a CAGA certified appraiser. Second, an extensive library for research on items customers bring in or want to puchase. Besides that, there's a clock repairman, a victrola repairman and a furniture restorer, all on site and ready to testify to the precision and detail of their work.

Besides the beautiful and well-made furniture, Owner Carolyn Martin has amassed a wonderful collection of fine glassware and china, linens, art glass, jewelry, christening gowns, clocks, and Civil War items.

We loved the Victorian victro-las— which, thanks to the talented repairman, really work— and the selection of Majolica, Depression glass and Victorian glassware.

To find it: 713 S. Main St. Georgetown, Texas 78626.
Phone: 512/869-3088.
Accepts: MC, Visa, Discover, and personal checks.
Hours: 10:00-6:00, seven days a week. Open most holidays.
Shipping: Available.
Notable: High-quality antiques, wonderful glassware collection.

1 **Our House to Your House Featuring Von Nash Interiors.** A motivational speaker for 22 years, Von Nash changed careers 10 years ago to do what she loved — decorating. Over

the years, while on speaking engagements across the country and abroad, she often stayed in private homes. At night, she would find herself consulting with the homeowners, helping them decorate.

Von decide to settle in the Hill Country and chose Georgetown as her home. She bought a building on the Georgetown square, built in the year 1874. At this location, in an upstairs office, the predecessor company to Texaco was formed. Since Von started her business in 1994, she has slowly but surely been investing all profits into restoring this historic structure.

Now, the building contains a 6,000-square-foot shopping area with custom designs mixed in with name brands. You'll find Seaton Glass, Yankee Candles, Heritage Lace, Aromatique and more in the gift area, and Von also carries a variety of lamps, furniture lines and antiques.

Astounding in their abundance are wallpaper and fabric samples, which allow customers to choose exactly what they want for special order. Custom window treatments and bedding are available, as well as custom iron furniture.

The shop also serves as Von's home base for her roving consulting service. Over the past 18 months, she has decorated more than 100 homes, small and large, in the Georgetown area. She prides herself in her knack for using professional design and color schemes to reflect the owner's personality — not the decorator's. She believes in using the customer's best-loved objects and blending in new items they want and can afford.

Her hourly design fee, plus an administrative fee for contractors, is an expense that pays off. Von says clients say she has actually saved them money — while giving them a satisfaction with their homes that they've never had before. Her design services are available by appointment.

Von's motto is that function is more important than fashion — but you can have both! No wonder her customers are so loyal.

To find it: 718 S. Austin Avenue, or write P.O. Box 865, Georgetown, Texas 78626, Phone: 512/869-0272.
Accepts: MC, Visa, Amex, Discover, and personal checks with proper ID.
Hours: 10 am. to 5 p.m. Tuesday-Saturday, closed Sunday and Monday.
Notable: 365 wallpaper books. 60,000 fabric samples. "If you need it, we will get it."

Every woman needs a role model, someone to encourage her to do great things.

Grace Jones had her father, W.R. "Willie" Rosanky, who taught her she could do anything she set her mind to.

Even when Jones, a teenaged college student, appeared at her rancher father's doorstep during World War II to ask whether she could join up with the Women Airforce Service Pilots (WASPs) to free up men for combat service, his answer was characteristic. Knowing his daughter had never before been inside an airplane, he told her, "I could do it, so I don't see why you couldn't do it."

Living her life by that credo led Jones into the skies as a WASP, and down fashion runways in New York and Japan. She stuck to what she wanted, so that even when she was "discovered" and wooed by a Hollywood producer/director, she declined. She was already doing "the most exciting thing in the world"— flying.

This vision led Jones back to Texas — Salado, to be exact—with perfect confidence. "Salado is magic," she has said. "If it's magic for me, then why wouldn't it be magic for anybody else?"

She came to Salado bearing haute couture. Her shop, Grace Jones of Salado, has acquired the status of a legend over the past 38 years for its chic elegance and gracious service. Sophisticated it may be, but it's welcoming, too. Jones loves giving tours of her beautiful, 1910 bank building.

Now, Jones likes to think that her bold life has inspired other ambitious young women to meet their own challenges with gusto. That she has been the role model who encourages them to venture beyond the expected to the world of their dreams.

Throughout her life experiences, Jones never consciously set out to be "famous"–or successful–she just lived life.

2 Rose Cottage Gifts and Antiques, Pink Rose Tearoom.

Did you ever want to get away from your same, old routine? Do you wish you could get together with some girlfriends for a chicken salad sandwich, with antique and gift shopping right at your disposal?

The Pink Rose Tearoom and Rose Cottage Gifts and Antiques not only offers a nice lunch in a Victorian atmosphere, but also shopping right

at hand.

The McLaurin family took over the tearoom in October of 1994. The four sisters can cook with a real Southern style. Every day, they prepare a chef's special and a soup of the day.

The regular menu includes the Pink Rose's famous sandwiches, made with fresh, homebaked bread. Chicken salad is a house specialty. It's made with delicious chicken, blended with grapes and almonds.

Also on the menu are entrees such as chicken spaghetti, pasta salad, stuffed tomato, croissant sandwiches and baked potatoes.

Any of these light lunches needs to be followed by a delicious homemade dessert. The Pink Rose offers delectable desserts made daily, including pies, cakes and cheesecakes. Just to tempt your sweet tooth, here's a sampling: Coconut Meringue Pie, Tollhouse Pie, Key Lime Pie, French Silk Pie, Chocolate Amaretto Pie and cheesecake.

After your delightful lunch and dessert, browse around Rose Cottage Gifts and Antiques. The gift selection comprises a wide variety, from children's books and tea sets to jewelry, glassware, candles and architectural pieces. Antique furniture, garlands and wreaths make the shop lovely, and also are for sale.

This spot is a great place for a party as well. The Pink Rose can accommodate groups of 15-20 for special events in a private room. Custom menus are available for bridal showers, anniversaries, birthdays and so forth, and the chefs will accommodate unique requests so that each party is special.

Whether you are browsing for gifts or antiques, having lunch or just stopping by for coffee and dessert, The Pink Rose Tea Room and Rose Cottage Gifts and Antiques will offer you the best in Southern hospitality. The friendly smiles and personalized service are as sweet as the dessert tray — and that's really sweet!

To find it: 102 North Main.
Phone: 254/947-9110.
Accepts: Visa, Amex, Discover, and personal checks with identification.
Hours: Gift Shop, 10:00-5:00; Tea Room, 11:00-3:00 weekdays and 11:00-5:00 weekends. Closed Tuesdays. Open holidays except Christmas Eve and Christmas Day, Thanksgiving and Easter.
Notable: Gift wrap free. Custom menus for special events such as birthday, anniversary, wedding shower.

1 **Heirlooms.** This two-story extravaganza of shopping offers the best of the past and present in one place.

The husband-and-wife team of Paul and Jean White started Heirlooms in 1995 aiming to pool their talents. She had a career in public relations and banking to her credit. His background was in sales. Together they created Heirlooms, a 7,500-square-foot store stocked with the best in gifts, apparel, jewelry, gourmet food, antiques and collectibles.

The building itself is an impressive structure with its clock tower and long gallery. But it's what's inside that's most appealing. Leave plenty of time for browsing, because the selection of wonderful products deserves close attention. You'll find decorative accessories for the home, unusual and beautiful clothing, jewelry, flavorful coffees, fragrant candles, gifts, florals, potpourri and more.

One of the many striking collections in Heirlooms is the Elsie

Massey Originals limited edition dolls. Displayed among beautiful table linens and ceramics, the dolls range from Victorian ladies to sweet baby dolls. Only 200 of each limited edition are manufactuctured.

Also noteworthy are the American traditional works by Austinite Bill Barriek; the landscapes and bluebonnet paintings of Peggy

Byars; the Texas Collection watercolors by Clifton artist George Boutwell; and the works of Salado native Gretchen Clasby.

Plus, shopping at Heirlooms is always relaxed and friendly. Paul, Jean, Cindy and Connie set out to create not only a collage of wonderful products and merchandise, but also to make the store known for its customer service and friendly attitude. We'd say they've succeeded.

To find it: 230 N. Main St., Salado, 76571.
Phone: 254/947-0336.
Accepts: MC, Visa, Amex, Discover. Personal checks.
Hours: Monday-Saturday 10 a.m. to 6 p.m. Sundays 11 a.m. to 5:30 p.m. Open holidays except Christmas, New Year's Day and Thanksgiving.
Notable: Complimentary coffee and goodies served on weekends. Wide selection of gifts.

4 **The Stagecoach Inn.** In years past, this Chisholm Trail stop welcomed Gen. George Custer and the notorious James brothers. Today, the lovely landmark's frontier heritage is preserved in a down-home atmosphere where you'll find the best in country food and comfortable accommodations.

To find it: Interstate 35, take exit 283 or 284.
Phone: 800/732-8994
Accepts: MC, Visa, Amex, Discover. Personal checks.
Hours: Seven days a week, 11 a.m. to 4 p.m. and 5-9 p.m.
Notable: Historic building and grounds. Wonderful, traditional Texas food. Inn's amenities and activities are numerous.

The Stagecoach Inn is steeped in history, lending a special flavor to a meal, an overnight stay or a business meeting in one of the well-equipped, modern conference rooms.

The two eateries' Texas meals are built around original farm and ranch recipes. Traditional favorites such as plate-size steaks and fried chicken join unique appetizers and desserts like tomato aspic and banana fritters — plus the tastiest hush puppies in Texas.

Car in Character
By Linda Dumont

3 **Salado Square.** This 19th Century brick building was disassembled in West Texas and reassembled in Salado by several local artists. Today it houses five shops and a restaurant.

Brownings: A family-owned restaurant, Brownings offers fresh, home-made sandwiches, quiches, casseroles, as well as beautiful desserts, all served in a homey, cozy dining room. Don't miss the fresh-baked bread or out-of-this world desserts.
To find it: No. 4 Salado Square, Main Street, Salado, Texas.
Phone: 254/947-8666.
Fax: 254/947-8675.
Accepts: MC, Visa. Personal checks with ID.
Hours: Daily 11 a.m. to 4 p.m.

Main Street Place: This newest addition to the square offers a collection of antiques and unusual furniture, lighting and accessories. Very personal service is provided by an uncommonly knowledgable staff.
To find it: No. 8 Salado Square.
Phone: 254/947-9908.
Accepts: Visa, Amex, MC, Discover.
Layaway available.
Hours: 10 a.m. to 5 p.m. daily.

Cio ... A Unique Ladies Boutique: Distinctive fashions and Brighton accessories make shopping at this designated Brighton Heart store a must. A full line of Brighton accesories, including handbags and shoes, makes Cio your Brighton headquarters. Fabulous fashions from Double D, Surya, and Telluride offer a unique shopping experience. Shopping is fun here in the friendly, comfortable atmosphere.

To find it: No. 3 Salado Square.
Phone: 254/947-0322.
Accepts: Visa, MC, Amex, Discover.
Layaway available.
Hours: Mondays-Saturdays 10 a.m. to 5 p.m., Sundays 1 p.m. to 5 p.m.

Magnolias on the Square: Reminiscent of an old-fashioned mercantile, Magnolias is an emporium of unique specialty shops. The large variety of different offerings includes a ladies' shoes boutique, a gift shop for pets and pet lovers, a country store with kitchen linens and Texas gifts ... 20 distinctive collections in all ... all under one roof.

To find it: No. 1 Salado Square.
Phone: 254/947-0323.
Accepts: MC, Visa, Discover, personal checks. Layaway available.
Hours: Mondays-Saturdays 10 a.m. to 5 p.m., Sundays 12-5 p.m.
Email: MagnoliaSq@aol.com.

Barnhill Britt: This gallery and showroom offers furniture and accessories handcrafted by local cabinetmaker John Barnhill and other Central Texas artisits. Art glass, hand-thrown pottery, reclaimed longleaf pine furniture and traditional redware are only a few of the fabulous things here.

To find it: No. 6 Salado Square.
Phone: 800/473-1494.
Accepts: MC, Visa, Discover, Amex. Personal checks with proper ID.
Hours: 10 a.m. to 5 p.m. Mondays to Saturdays, 12 to 5 p.m. Sunday. Open holidays except Thanksgiving and Christmas.
Online: www.barnhillbritt.com.

Carden's: Gifts, home decor, children's books, body lotions and scents, and stationery are only a few of the wonderful things you'll find in this friendly shop. Caspari paper products are on hand to dress up your parties. Relgious books and stationery are available, as are framed prints, rugs and quilts.

To find it: No. 5 Salado Square.
Phone: 254/947-0300.
Accepts: MC, Visa, personal checks with proper ID.
Hours: 10 a.m. to 5 p.m. Mondays to Saturdays, 12 to 5 p.m. Sunday.

2 **Daryl Howard.** Trained in Tokyo with a master woodblock printmaker Hodaka Yoshida, Daryl Howard creates her prints in a studio near Dripping Springs, using the traditional Japanese methods. She also makes collages on metallic-leafed boards, each one-of-a-kind. Though her work has been exhibited in juried shows and museums all over the world, you need only travel to her studio to view her work. She will come to offices or residences to help clients place her artwork, and also creates collages by commission. A catalog of work is available.

To find it: 14100 Nutty Brown Road.
Phone: 512/288-4744.
E-mail: howard@jump.net.
Website: www.daryl/howard.com.
Accepts: MC, Visa, Amex. Personal checks.
Hours: By appointment.
Notable: Woodblock prints created using traditional Japanese methods. Unusual, mixed media collages.

1 **Cowgirls & Lace and Le Ragge Ruggs.** In this relaxed and friendly Hill Country atmosphere, you'll find everything you need to carry out your decorating vision. Cowgirls & Lace offers a tremendous selection of fabrics, furniture and accessories to fit a wide range of personal styles. Whether you like the rustic ranch look or a more formal French Country milieu—or anything in between—you'll find just the right pieces here.

The huge array of fabrics includes a host of Ralph Lauren designs and many 100-inch-plus widths; you can make your selection and have Cowgirls & Lace stitch up custom bed coverings and window treatments. You can use your custom-made linens to grace a new wrought-iron bed, and add a coordi-

nating upholstered chair and an array of throw pillows. Furniture lines include Corsican Metal Beds, Double D, and Old Hickory Tannery.

No room is complete without special accessories, so Cowgirls & Lace also carries candles, artwork and frames, as well as other home accessories to round out the decorating selection. There's also a collection of gifts, from stationery to toys for the kids.

To find it: In Trailhead Market, Hwy 290 West in Dripping Springs.
Phone: 512/858-4186, 894-0350.
Accepts: MC, Visa, Amex. Personal checks with ID.
Hours: Monday-Saturday, 10 a.m. to 6 p.m.; Sunday, 1-6 p.m.
Notable: Many unique offerings to personalize your home. Extensive selection of home decorating fabrics.

Apparel

Art Galleries

Bookstores

Entertainment

Flower Shops

Gifts/Antiques cont.

Home Furnishings

Jewelry

Lodging

Professional Services

Professional Services cont.

Restaurants

Restaurants cont.

Success Stories

Attractions

Notes:

Notes:

Linda Dumont

The art you see on our cover and throughout this book is the work of Austin artist Linda Dumont.

Linda is an emerging national artist whose home and studio have been in Austin since 1984. She has been a practicing painter since 1981, when she graduated from the School of the Museum of Fine Arts, Boston.

Dumont's work has been shown nationally, and her specially commissioned paintings grace corporate facilities in major Texas cities. Most notably, Dumont had a solo museum show in 1996 at the McAllen International Museum. A five-canvas ensemble commissioned by Motorola, entitled "It all Happens at Dimensions of One Micron Or Less," hangs in the company's Ed Bluestein/Austin facility. A pair of 11-foot paintings by Dumont has been installed at Southwestern University in Georgetown. She executed wall art for the Austin Children's Museum's Robo-City, and her unique interpretation of the Alamo is the focal point of IXC Corporation's executive conference room. She also has lent her special eye to several commissioned interpretations of the Austin skyline and the Texas Capitol.

Outside Texas, individuals and corporations in more than 20 states have collected Dumont's work, including 12 paintings in Houston-Effler Partnership's collection in Boston, work in office buildings on the New York Harbor, canvases in the private collections of executives of General Mills and Viacom-CBS, and an 11-foot painting commissioned for an office building lobby at Long Beach Marina, California.

"I work with paint as a dancer works with motion"
Linda Dumont, 1993

"...and the lyrical oils of Linda Dumont: what oils would do if they could paint themselves."
Critic Bejou Merry, in Significant Artists 1987

For additional information regarding art showings and commissioned work, contact Natalie Rupert at 521-345-9804.